WINGS OF
COURAGE

Translated and adapted by
PHILIPPA PEARCE
from a story by George Sand

Illustrated by Hilary Abrahams

Hodder
Children's
Books

a division of Hodder Headline plc

First published in Great Britain in 1982
Penguin Books Ltd

This edition published in Great Britain in 1998
by Hodder Children's Books

10 9 8 7 6 5 4 3 2 1

A Catalogue record for this book is available
from the British Library

ISBN 0 340 71510 3

Typeset by Avon Dataset Ltd, Bidford-on-Avon, Warks
Printed and bound in Great Britain by
Clays Ltd, St Ives plc

Hodder and Stoughton
A division of Hodder Headline PLC
338 Euston Road
London NW1 3BH

George Sand's

WINGS OF COURAGE

Other titles in the Hodder Classics series:

Peter Pan
J. M. Barrie

Whistle Down the Wind
Mary Hayley Bell

The Incredible Journey
Sheila Burnford

A Little Princess
The Railway Children
The Secret Garden
Frances Hodgson Burnett

Children of the New Forest
Captain Marryat

Anne of Green Gables
L. M. Montgomery

In 1872 George Sand made up the story of Clopinet to please her two little granddaughters, Aurore and Gabrielle. She dedicated it to them.

This English version is dedicated to
HILARY ABRAHAMS
whose happy idea it was.

ACKNOWLEDGEMENT

In the translation and adaptation of this story, I owe much gratitude to James Cadbury for his expert ornithological advice. Any errors still to be found are the responsibility of the original story-teller. Readers are referred to the explanatory note 'George Sand and Her Birds' at the end of this book.

CONTENTS

1   The Boy and the Tailor   1
2   Escape   9
3   The Sea   15
4   The Black Cow   25
5   The House on the Shore   33
6   The Hide-away   43
7   Three Feathers   53
8   The Tailor Again   65
9   Night Herons   73
10 Clopinet Goes Home   81
11 At the Apothecary's   91
12 At the Great House   103
13 A Night of Storm   113
14 The Castaway   125
15 Goodbye to Clopinet   137
    Afterword: George Sand and her Birds   147

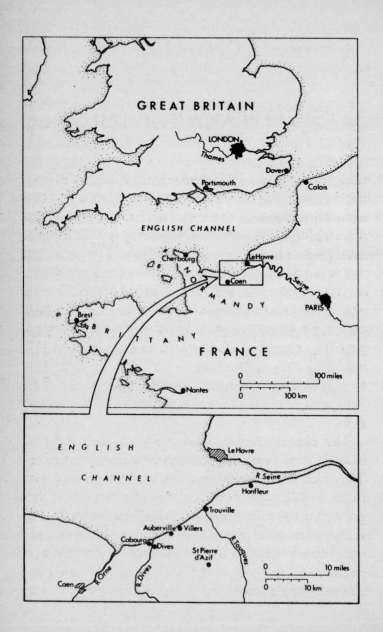

1

THE BOY AND THE TAILOR

Once upon a time, in Normandy, some ten miles from the sea, there lived a certain farmer and his wife. Their nearest village was the tiny hamlet of Saint Pierre d'Azif. They were well-off, for country people in those days; they worked hard and spent little.

Those days were towards the end of the eighteenth century. At that time and in that part of France, farming was very simple. As far as the eye could see over a flat, open countryside, there was nothing but pasture for cows and yet more pasture for cows; apple trees and yet more apple trees. And every so often a little half-timbered farmhouse with its farmyard and stick-yard and little garden.

In just such a farmhouse lived Farmer Doucy and his wife.

The Doucys had a good many children, who all helped on the farm. The children were like their parents. They were hard workers, not fast workers; they were set in their ways, and never dreamt of other ones; they grumbled, but only at the weather. Their one ambition, as they grew older, was to save a little money here and a little money there, so that in the end they would have enough to buy a plot of land and farm it. They wanted cows and apple trees.

But not Clopinet. The child was nicknamed that because of a lameness in one leg that made him clop along unevenly as he walked. All the same, he was sturdy and red-cheeked like his brothers and sisters. He worked on the farm like them – but he didn't want to. He wasn't lazy, and he didn't mean to be disobedient to his parents. But he had got this strange idea into his head that he must go to sea. He would have been hard put to it to explain exactly what *going to sea* meant, however, if anyone had asked him. But no one was interested.

Clopinet was only ten years old when the idea took possession of him, and this is how it came about.

Clopinet had an uncle, his mother's brother, who, as a boy, had gone to sea on a merchant-ship and so seen the world. This sailor-uncle had now settled down on the coast at Trouville. From here he used to visit his Doucy relations from time to time; and he would spin them yarns of his travels and the marvels he had seen. He told tall stories; but Clopinet believed them all. He was dazzled. He began to dream of travelling to wonderful, far-distant places. He longed and longed to go to sea – although he had never seen the sea, and hardly knew what it was.

Yet the sea was so close: the boy could have clop-clopped his way there without much difficulty. But Clopinet's father did not want him to get any taste for travel. In those days, country people never went from home unless they had to, on business; and Clopinet was not old enough to do farm-business for his father. His job was to stay at home and herd the cows.

Oh, how tired he was of cows! He had to drive them to pasture, and then stay with them. The other children would have settled down contentedly to play – making market-baskets from the rushes that grew by the brook or building tiny farmhouses from mud and twigs. But not Clopinet. He only gazed up into the clouds and watched the birds that flew by on their way to the sea, or from it.

'Lucky them!' he said to himself. 'They have wings and can fly wherever they please. They see the world and the wonders of it. They are never bored.'

He watched the birds so constantly that he soon knew them by their flight, however high they were flying. He knew their ways of travelling together: how the cranes flew in arrow-formation, the better to cut through the winds of the upper air; how the starlings

flew in a thick flock; and how the wild geese followed one after another in line at exact intervals. He loved to see the migrant birds coming. He tried to run as fast as they flew, but in vain. He had hardly taken ten steps before they had passed overhead and then out of sight.

Perhaps because of his lameness or perhaps because he was naturally timid, Clopinet hardly ventured from home. He had great curiosity, but not the courage to satisfy it.

One day his sailor-uncle came on a visit, and Clopinet talked of going back with him to see the sea – if his father would let him.

Farmer Doucy laughed. 'You?' he jeered. 'You'd better keep your mouth shut! You can't walk properly, and you're scared of everything. I warn you, brother-in-law: pay no attention to our Chicken-heart here. Last year he hid all one day in the stick-yard because a chimney-sweep went by with a sooty face and he thought it was the Devil! He squeals when he sees the tailor coming to make our clothes for us, and just because he's hunchbacked! He only needs a dog to growl, a cow to stare, an apple to fall, and he's off! Why, you could say he was born with wings of fear growing from his shoulders!'

'Oh, that will change,' answered Uncle Laquille, the sailor. 'Children may be born with wings of fear; but, as they grow older, other wings sprout.'

Clopinet was mystified by this. 'I haven't any wings,' he said. 'Father was joking. But perhaps wings would grow, if I went to sea . . .'

'If wings grow at sea,' said Farmer Doucy, 'then your

uncle should have some, shouldn't he? Tell him to show them to you!'

'I have them when I need them,' the sailor replied with dignity. 'I need wings of courage when I have to go into danger.'

Clopinet was much struck by these words of his uncle, and never forgot them.

But Farmer Doucy wanted to take his brother-in-law down a peg. 'I don't deny you have these wings when it's a question of duties at sea,' he said. 'But what about when you get home again? You're not so high and mighty then – your wife clips your wings for you then, I'll warrant!'

Everyone knew that Aunt Laquille ruled her husband and her household. Clopinet's mother was the exact opposite: meek and obedient to her husband in everything. And so she never dared speak up for Clopinet and his strange idea, because she knew her husband disapproved. Farmer Doucy declared that a sailor's life was much too hard for a boy with a lame leg. Nor would Clopinet ever make a farmer, he said.

What then?

The boy must be apprenticed to tailoring. It was a very respectable trade.

The day came for the travelling tailor's yearly visit to the Doucy family. Farmer Doucy welcomed him: 'Well, friend, and how's old Left-hand-thread?' (That was the tailor's nick-name: he was left-handed and sewed with his needle in the opposite way to everyone else.) 'This time we've no tailoring work for you; but we've a little lad who'd like to learn your trade. I know the customs

of apprenticeship: I'm ready to pay you a little something in the usual way. I can't afford much; but a strong
boy's going to be very useful to you. A year from now,
and he'll be helping you and running all your errands.
He'll be as good as a servant, and well worth his keep.'

'And how much is your *little something*, pray?' asked
the tailor. He cast a deliberately careless, disdainful
glance at the cowering boy. Old Left-hand-thread was
far too cunning to show any eagerness for this human
merchandise.

The farmer and the tailor began to bargain.

The prospect of a lifetime of scissoring and sewing
appalled Clopinet. As for the master to whom he was
being sold – he hardly dared look at him. The tailor was
hunched in both shoulders, squinting in both eyes, lame
in both legs. If he could have been untwisted and
stretched out on a table, he would have made a tall man;
but his body seemed to have been broken in pieces and
then stuck badly together again at the corners. He was
no taller than Clopinet himself, who wasn't big for his
age. (By now he was twelve.) Old Left-hand-thread
must have been at least fifty. His head was long and
yellow and bald, and looked like some gigantic cucum-
ber. He was dressed in the filthy rags and tatters of
clothing that his customers had discarded – stuff that
would have been thrown out on to the muck-heap, if he
had not begged it for his own use. But the most
repulsive things about him were his feet and hands,
disproportionately long and horribly, horribly nimble.
With his spindly arms and bow legs, he yet worked and
walked faster than anyone else. The eye could hardly

follow the flash of his great needle as he sewed, or the cloud of dust that swirled after him as he scythed his way over the ground when he ran.

Clopinet had seen old Left-hand-thread often, and always he had shrunk from him. Today the sight of him filled the boy with panic. He wanted to escape, to run right away. Then he remembered the wings of fear that he had been jeered at for having on his shoulders. He was terrified, but he stayed where he was.

And now the dreadful bargain was struck. Farmer Doucy and the tailor shook hands on it, and then drank to it, clinking jolly mugs of Normandy cider.

Clopinet's mother knew what came next. Without a word she slipped away to begin packing for her poor child, whom the tailor was to take from her for three whole years.

2

ESCAPE

Until that moment Clopinet had not fully taken in what was about to happen. He had not believed that his father would really hand him over to the tailor. But now the bargain had been struck. Now he saw his mother going from him with face averted to hide her tears. Now he knew.

He sprang after his mother to implore her to help him, to save him.

Too late! The tailor shot out an arm and seized him as a spider seizes a fly. He swung him up on to his back, with the boy's legs pulled to the front and clutched tightly there. 'Right!' he said to Farmer Doucy. 'I'll be off now! His mother can blubber to her heart's content. She'll cry less when he's not there, anyway – out of sight, out of mind, eh? But see that she packs up his things, and send them on to me tomorrow at Dives. I'll be working there for three days. As for you, boy, if you don't hold your noise, I'll cut out your tongue! Do you see the big scissors that hang from my belt here? Oh, they're sharp – sharp!'

'Don't be too hard on the lad,' said Clopinet's father. 'He's not a bad boy, really. He'll serve you well.'

'Don't you worry, I'll see to that,' said the tailor. 'And don't start getting sentimental, or I swear I won't take the brat off your hands at all. You're paying little enough money for the apprenticeship, as it is.'

'At least, let me say a proper good-bye to him,' said Farmer Doucy. 'After all, my child is leaving home for good . . .'

'Rubbish!' said the tailor. 'You'll see him again soon enough. I'll be bringing him back here to work with me some time, shan't I? So keep your hands off him now! He's mine now! And we're off!'

So saying, Left-hand-thread skipped out of the farmhouse door and began swiftly threading his way through the apple trees with Clopinet on his back. His little prisoner tried to cry out, but the child's teeth were chattering with terror and his voice choked in his throat. He managed to twist his body round for one last look at the home he was leaving. He saw his mother, who had rushed to the farmhouse door, with imploring

arms outstretched. Through his sobs he called her:
'Mother!' At that she would have started after him, but
her husband held her back. She struggled in vain, then
turned pale as death, and would have fallen to the
ground but for François, the eldest son of the Doucy
family. He caught her in his arms; and, while he
supported her, he shouted oaths after the tailor and
shook his fist in fury.

Left-hand-thread only laughed – a hideous sound like
the teeth of a saw on stone. He quickened his pace, that
monstrous, nightmarish stride which none could follow.

Clopinet thought that he had seen his mother die
before his very eyes. Nothing now could save him. He
wished only that he could die, too. His head fell forward
upon the tailor's shoulder, and he lost consciousness.

The tailor had left his wretched little donkey grazing
in the Doucys' meadow. He dumped Clopinet on its
back and gave the beast a great kick to start it trotting.
Off they went in the direction of the coast, and did not
stop until they had covered nearly ten miles. Now they
were among the dunes; and here the tailor halted his
donkey and lay down to take a nap. He did not bother
about the child, who had toppled to the ground. He did
not even bother to wonder whether he were asleep or ill.

When Clopinet opened his eyes, he thought at first
that he was alone. He lifted his head a little and looked
about him. He was amazed: he did not recognize this
place, and it was unlike anywhere he had ever known
before, or dreamt of. He lay in a hollow lined with thick,
coarse turf which grew in great tussocks over the uneven
ground. Here and there, all about, the ground seemed to

have been drawn up into fantastic peaks and points; or rather, the grey clay-like marl of which the dunes consisted had been worn and torn by weather, leaving these strange formations. Dunes and cliffs of marl stretched all along the coast in that part of Normandy; and the coast-road, such as it was, went along the middle of them. A traveller who took this path through the dunes might never see the sea, although it lay so near.

After that first astonishment, Clopinet remembered – and his heart contracted at the memory – how he had been carried off by the tailor. Then he felt a rush of joy at the thought that his kidnapper must have abandoned him here. From here all he had to do was to find his way home.

Home! In an instant he was on his feet and taking the first steps along the path that stretched so plainly, so invitingly before him. Then he froze in terror. Only two paces from him lay Left-hand-thread, one eye closed in sleep, the other watching his every movement. The donkey was cropping the grass a little way off.

Clopinet dropped to the ground again and lay there as still as he could for the frightened heartbeats that shook his small body.

Suddenly and distinctly he heard a strange sound. Had a dog growled? Or was it a pig's grunt? Or the cawing of a crow? Cautiously he raised his head to look about him again. He looked towards the tailor, and realized that what he had heard was a snore. Left-hand-thread was asleep and snoring, with one eye open. Though Clopinet did not know it, this was quite usual with him: one eye was blind and always stayed open. But, for all that, the

tailor was asleep now – deeply asleep, for he was tired, and
the afternoon was drowsy with warmth.

Clopinet got up on to his hands and knees and
crawled towards the tailor. He was still terrified by the
dreadful eye that glared at him so unblinkingly; but he
crawled closer and closer. He raised his hand and passed
it to and fro before the eye, and the eye never altered. So
the eye was sightless.

He turned about and crept away as fast as he could.
He took the path out of the grassy hollow, only to find
himself in a similar hollow, but larger. The path led
directly across it. He paused now to take his sabots off
his feet and leave them, so that he could run more freely.

He ran in his jerky, clop-clop way for some time; then
he left the path abruptly. He launched himself among

the long grasses, scrambling up and down steep slopes with the panic rush of a hunted hare. Tangles of bushes and plants met over his head; but still he ran and ran.

Then, gradually, he began to think more calmly, to reason. Soon the tailor would be looking everywhere for him, and the shaking of leaves and grasses might betray his presence. At the thought, he halted at once. There and then he huddled down under the thickest cover of leaves and waited motionless, silent, hardly daring to breathe.

His stratagem succeeded. The tailor slept as long as he needed, and then woke up. He saw at once that his prisoner had escaped, and cast about to find him. He found the sabots on the path, but did not trouble to pick them up. Instead, for a little way, he followed the print of Clopinet's bare feet still going along the same path, in the direction of Dives. That made him snigger: 'What a fool of a boy! He must think he's running home, when all the time he's on the road I was taking him anyway! I shall soon catch up with him; and then—!'

The tailor fetched his donkey and began to drive it along the way that Clopinet had taken. He did not notice when the footprints ceased, where Clopinet had left the path. He heard no sound, he saw no movement that might have warned him that he was passing Clopinet in his hiding-place, instead of following him. On the tailor went, skimming over the ground, with his great twisted legs moving like scythes at work on some horrid harvest.

On he went, and the faster he hurried, the further he left Clopinet behind him, free.

3

THE SEA

Night was falling before Clopinet felt it safe to come out of his hiding-place. Even then, he listened intently. The mild spring evening, hazy with mist, seemed absolutely still. Then he became aware of an unfamiliar, odd sound.

What could it be? Perhaps these were the footsteps of the tailor, beneath which the earth itself cried out in protest? Or was the sound like the tearing of cloth? And again his mind flew to the tailor, who ripped his cloth before he started on it with his terrible shears.

But the sound came again and again . . .

No louder, no softer . . .

No faster, no slower . . .

No nearer . . .

Never ceasing . . .

The sound was the sea breaking on the shore; but Clopinet did not know that.

Now, gaining a little courage, he stood on tiptoe and poked his head above the concealing bushes. He peered through the dusk.

Was there anyone else about in that lonely place?

No one.

But he beheld a great curve of dunes, whose juttingsout and foldings-in he could not see properly in the failing light.

The whole appeared to him like a huge rampart, breached here and there into emptiness.

That emptiness held the sea; but, again, Clopinet had not the slightest inkling of such a thing. The evening mist hid the horizon from him, so that he could not distinguish it from the sky. He marvelled that there were not only stars in the sky above, but also most strange luminosities below. Was this some kind of summer lightning? But why below?

How could such wonders possibly be understood by someone who had seen nothing of the world, not even a river of any size, not even a baby mountain?

By someone who had never seen the sea?

For a little while Clopinet wandered aimlessly among the bushes and tussocks of the dune. He was frightened, and hungry, and very tired. 'I must – I *must* find somewhere to sleep,' he told himself. 'Then, at first light, I can seek out someone to tell me the way home. I must go home to make sure my mother isn't dead.' He wept at the thought.

He dared not settle in the first place he found, for fear of being surprised there by the tailor. He imagined his ruffian of a master still beating about for his recapture. He could not get far enough away from the path by which the tailor might return to hunt him out.

So he decided to make his way down from the dune. He soon realized that the descent was going to be far more difficult than he had thought. The side of the dune was not like a wall down which he could have let himself drop or slide. No, there was yet more broken ground, deeply cracked, and spiky as a horse-chestnut. Those substantial-seeming spikes crumbled under his hands when he tried to cling to them. He came across deep fissures hidden by grasses and thorn bushes, and he was always afraid of falling down them. Some he could not avoid in time: they had water in the bottom, but not very much, fortunately.

The darkness of oncoming night and the loneliness of the place and the dangers of the treacherous terrain – everything joined together to fill Clopinet with dread. After all, he had never experienced anything like this in his whole life before; and he was only a little boy, lame in one leg.

Finally he gave up the descent. He would go back.

Going up again was even worse. The upper ground had at least been dried by the sun and a little held together by the thick vegetation; but the sides of the so-called rock were wet and slippery. He could find no sure foothold. Meanwhile, great lumps of the marl itself broke away, and here and there sent tumbling down a shower of lesser pieces.

Clopinet was soon worn out. He gave himself up for lost. He would not have been much surprised if wolves had come along just to finish him off.

In despair he threw himself down on a thick cushion of moss, determined to sleep if he could, in order to cheat his hunger. But he fell asleep only to dream that he was slipping – falling; and some creature that ran lightly over him – perhaps a fox, perhaps a hare – so terrified him that he sprang up again. He fled without

knowing where, and even at the risk of falling down a
crevasse and drowning in deep water at the bottom.

He no longer knew reality from dream, and did not
recognize again things he had seen plainly by daylight.
He sped from one grassy hollow to another, and came
again to those great crests of dune that had so astonished him earlier. Now he took them to be giants that
reared their heads against him. Every black bush now
seemed a wild beast, crouching to pounce on him. His
head swam with lunatic thoughts and with memories of
things long forgotten. Once in his hearing, his sailor-
uncle had said: 'When you give yourself up to the sea,
the land will have nothing more to do with you.' Those
words now echoed ominously in his head. 'I've longed
for the sea,' he told himself, 'and now the earth hates me.
Everywhere it cracks open under my feet, and draws
itself up into heights to fall on me and crush me! Oh, I
am lost – lost! I don't know where the sea is, that might
be my friend. I don't know where my home is – or
whether I even have a home. Lost – all lost!'

While these thoughts were crowding into his mind,
he heard a strange sound coming towards him in the air,
and then beginning to pass overhead. A myriad of
plaintive little voices seemed to appeal for help. Surely
these were not the cries of birds, but the voices of
children like himself – and like himself unhappy, grieving! He cried aloud: 'This way! Come this way! I am
here – here!' He wanted to be with them, whoever they
were. They would be company for him in sadness. He
would no longer be alone.

The voices continued to pass overhead: there were so

many that their passage lasted several minutes. During that time, they took no notice of Clopinet, although he pleaded with them, sad voice calling to sad voices. At last, the cries came less often, as the band went into the distance. Now the only ones to pass overhead were solitary, belated voices. They seemed to call upon the others, in tones of anguish, to wait for them.

All this time Clopinet had been running, but quite without managing to keep up with the voices above him. When he heard what seemed to be the last of them, he became desperate. These invisible companions in misfortune had been a kind of comfort to him; now he faced again the horrors of solitude. He cried aloud: 'Don't leave me! Take me with you!'

At that same moment, while he ran, he made a tremendous effort as if to open great wings. Either his passionate longing made miracle-wings grow, or what happened next was a dream brought about by the light-headedness of hunger. Whichever it was, he seemed to feel himself rising, flying . . .

Up he went into a pearly greyness, through which he thought he could distinguish little black arrow-shapes that flew always ahead of him. But soon he could see nothing but fog. He called again for the voices to wait for him, but in vain. They flew faster than he could. They were lost among the clouds.

Then Clopinet seemed to feel his wings grow weary and lose their power. His flight slowed, became laboured. He began to come down–down − without falling, but without being able to stop himself − down − down − to the foot of the dune.

At first, even then, he could still think only of flying. Frantically and uselessly he flapped his arms again and again. But not for long. The sight that now met his eyes drove all other thoughts from him.

He had landed on fine, soft sand. The night was still misty, but the mist was not thick enough to hide from him strange presences nearby – great rounded shapes, whitish in colour. At first he took them to be apple trees in bloom. He looked more carefully, and went close enough to touch those that were nearest to him. He realized that these were huge boulders such as he had seen high up on the dune. They must have rolled down from there, probably long ago, on to the sands.

The sands were smooth, clean, beautiful. Every day the tide came up and covered them, washing away any mud that fell down from the marly dunes and cliffs. And a thousand little rills of fresh water seeped through the sands and washed them all over again, and then lost themselves – without sound or bubble – in the great salt water beyond.

But as yet the tide was not at its height. Clopinet heard, without understanding, the sound of the approaching waves; but he could not see beyond the pallor of the wet sands. Their expanse, he noticed, was broken by a number of *things* – each one a black mass more or less large, more or less rounded. There were a great many of them – a whole herd, one might say.

Clopinet felt no fear; he gazed at the motionless shapes only with wonder. Yes, they lay there like some herd of enormous, sleeping animals. He wanted to look at them more closely. He went over the sands until he was near enough to touch one. It was no animal, but rock — rock just like the ones he had already seen. But why should this rock be black, while those at the foot of the dune were white? He touched it again, and this time brought away in his fingers something like an enormous bunch of black grapes. He was hungry, so he bit into it: he felt between his teeth the hardness of shellfish. But his teeth were strong, and went on biting, and he found he was eating excellent little mussels. He took out his knife and began to prise open the shells. He must satisfy his hunger, and there were plenty of mussels for that. They coated the whole rock, blackening it all over.

When Clopinet had eaten, he felt himself quite restored — restored, too, to common sense. He no longer thought that he had had wings, and flown. No, he must have been rolling gently down the slopes of marl, when he had thought himself flying through the clouds.

And now he climbed on to the biggest of the great black rocks, in order to see into the distance. Again he saw the long flashing to and fro of those pale lights that he had seen before. They seemed to skim as low as the earth itself.

What could they be? He remembered his uncle once saying that the water of the sea often glowed with a white fire during the night.

What he was seeing must be the sea!

The sea was very near to him; and it was coming ever nearer. Its advance was so gradual, its motion so regular, its sound so monotonous, that Clopinet was hardly aware of this gentle invasion. From the top of his black rock, he watched without misgiving as the water came forward, and then went back; advanced, retreated; folded over on itself in slow undulation; rose slowly up again, only slowly to fall again . . .

Again and again . . .

Until again the wave crept forward and at last spent itself upon the shore, with that small sound, sharp yet sweet, that charms the listener on a still night, and soothes his senses to sleep.

And Clopinet could not resist that sound. After all, the time was about ten o'clock in the evening, and he had never in his life stayed awake so late before. His bed of rock and shell-fish was not exactly soft; but when you're tired out, as Clopinet was, you sleep anywhere.

For a little while he lay there awake. He fixed his heavy eyes on the silvery sheet of water that lay before him. Still it crept over the sand towards him: one little wave advanced at the very instant that another was retreating, and each advancing wave brought the silvery expanse just a little nearer . . .

And nearer . . .

Nothing is less immediately alarming than that gentle, treacherous invasion by the rising tide.

Clopinet saw quite clearly that the strip of sand in front of his rock was narrowing, and that little ripples would soon be washing the base of it. That did not trouble him: he only marvelled at the beauty of the ripples, white-topped with foam.

So this was the sea! He was seeing it, he could touch it at last. It did not seem very big to him: he could not see beyond the first five or six waves. After that, there was only darkness and mist.

Nor did it seem that there could come any harm from the sea. He remembered that his sailor-uncle had often spoken of the sea as a person – a woman, a great lady – to be treated with respect. That reminded Clopinet that he had not so far greeted her, and that was a discourtesy. By now he was almost overwhelmed with sleep, yet he managed politely to raise his woollen cap to his new friend, the sea. Then he let his head fall upon his outstretched arm and, with his cap still in his hand, he fell deeply asleep.

4

THE BLACK COW

Two hours later the tide was at the full. Clopinet was woken by the thundering of the sea all about him. The waves were beating on his rock with such force that it seemed to tremble under the onslaught.

His rock? He could no longer see the very rock upon which he crouched, for the boiling foam that encircled it.

In his simplicity he thought he could at least leave the rock by the way he had come; but there was just as much water on that side as elsewhere. The other black rocks had already disappeared from view under the water; and the greedy flood had reached the white rocks and seemed intent upon swallowing them, too.

He tried to lower his legs into the water, to see how deep it was. He could not feel the bottom, but he did feel with certainty that if he once let go of his rock, the waves would take him.

He shut his eyes against the coming of what seemed certain death. No earthly power could save him now.

And then, suddenly, he heard above him the little voices that had called to him on the dune. Against all reason, he took heart at the sound. Surely he had really flown once, when he had come down from the dune to the shore . . . Surely he could fly again . . .

He called to the invisible voices, matching his cry to theirs. This time they did not disregard him. He heard them wheeling above him, calling as if to him alone, waiting impatiently for him.

He strained upwards – upwards – and felt himself rising. He flew – he flew! Not high, but skimming the tops of the waves, gliding to and fro, returning perhaps for a moment's rest on his island-rock, then off again, gliding, flitting, dipping into the sea itself. In this last he found the greatest delight. The sea-water felt warm to his body, and he could keep himself afloat on it without effort, as if he had been born to this element. Then he felt he must see under the surface of the sea. He folded his wings and plunged head downwards. He seemed to enter a white fire that did not burn; the sea blazed white around him.

At last, he began to tire, and came back to his rock to rest. There he lay, unafraid now, listening to the beating waves and the childlike voices that still called above him. After a while, he fell asleep, lulled by the sounds of the sea.

When he woke again, all was changed. The sun was rising through a silvery mist, already melting away here and there along the horizon. A freshening wind rippled the greenness of the now-distant waters. Towards the sunrise this colouring changed to pink and lilac. Minute by minute the horizon became more sharply defined; and the rock on which Clopinet had slept was high enough for him at last to realize the vastness of the sea.

But the sea had gone so far away!

Now, by daylight, he wanted to see it close to. He left his rock and ran out over the sands, splashing through the pools left behind by the tide, not stopping for anything, until he had reached the sea and waded in it.

Along the sea's edge he began to collect a great number of shellfish, all pretty and all good to eat. Then he went back to where the dunes began, to drink from the little streams there. The water tasted brackish, but less bitter than the sea-water he had sucked from his fingers.

He was happy, deeply happy, to be at last by the sea, that had haunted so many of his dreams. He no longer thought of going home. He almost forgot what had happened only yesterday. He began to roam to and fro along the sea-shore, looking at everything, touching everything, trying to take everything in.

Far out at sea, he saw sailing boats. He knew what they were because he could make out the men aboard and the sails filled by the wind. He even saw an ocean-going ship on the horizon. He took it for a church, at first; but then he realized that it moved just like the smaller boats. His heart beat fast. So this was a ship – one of those floating mansions in which his uncle had made his voyages! Clopinet longed to be aboard, to sail beyond the grey horizon, to the sea's end.

The tailor was quite out of his thoughts, when the fear of him returned abruptly: Clopinet saw someone in the distance, walking along the sea-shore, in his direction. But he was soon reassured to see that the man was quite ordinary in appearance. And he thought he recognized him: his elder brother, François – the very one who, the day before, had shaken an angry fist at the tailor. François hated the tailor and loved Clopinet dearly.

And it *was* he! Clopinet rushed to meet him and throw himself into his arms.

François hugged him. 'But where've you been?' he asked. 'Where've you come from? It's only seven o'clock in the morning, and you haven't come from Dives. So where've you spent the night?'

'Over there, on that big black rock,' said Clopinet.

'What! On the Great Cow?'

'It's not a cow, silly! It's a rock, really and truly!'

'Of course, I know it's a rock! But don't you know that those rocks are called the Black Cows? And where were you when the tide came in?'

'What do you mean?'

'I mean, what about the sea's coming right up here, and right up even to the rocks they call the White Cows?'

'Oh, yes, that did happen. But the sea-spirits prevented my drowning.'

'Clopinet! Don't be silly! There aren't such things as sea-spirits. There may be spirits on land, but that's another matter . . .'

'I tell you, sea-spirits came to my help,' Clopinet said doggedly.

'You actually saw them?'

'No, but I heard them. And here I am as proof: I slept safe and sound with the sea all round me.'

'Then you had tremendous luck, that's all I can say! Of course, I know that the Great Cow, being the biggest, is the one the tide never quite covers *when the sea is calm*. But if there'd been the slightest squall of wind, the waves would have come right up over the rock, and you'd have been finished, little 'un.'

'Pooh! I know how to swim and dive and fly low over the tops of the waves – oh, it's all been such fun, François!'

'Come now, Clopinet! You know you're talking nonsense! Your clothes aren't even wet. Now, eat up the bread I've brought you, and drink up the cider from my flask. Then you can tell me – calmly and sensibly, mind! – how you escaped from that brute of a tailor. For I can see you really have got from under his evil claws.'

Clopinet told him exactly what had happened.

'Well,' said François, 'I'm glad he didn't have you at his mercy for long, for he's a really bad man. I know for a fact that he's killed apprentices in the past by beating them and starving them to death. But will Father listen to what I tell him? He's even persuaded Mother that I've a spite against the man and made the whole thing up! You know how afraid she is of Father, and how she goes along with him in everything. Yesterday she cried her eyes out after you'd gone, and wouldn't touch a crumb at supper-time; but this morning she listened to what Father had to say, and believed him. Between them they decided that you would have got over any unhappiness by now, and would be quite all right under your new master. There was absolutely no way of persuading them to the contrary.

'So, if you go home now, Father will just give you a good hiding and take you back himself this very evening to Dives. The tailor never stays long in any one place, but he's due for two more days there – Mother

won't be able to stand up for you; she'll only cry.

'If you take my advice, you'll go and seek out our Uncle Laquille at Trouville. Ask him to get you taken on as a cabin boy in the Navy. You'll be happy then. You've always wanted that.'

But Clopinet was cast down. 'No one will want me as a sailor,' he said. 'Father said so: someone with a lame leg isn't a real man; all you can make of him is a tailor.'

'What wicked nonsense!' said François angrily. 'And, anyway, you can't be as lame as all that, since you've been running about barefoot for most of the night in these wilds. Are you any the worse for it?'

'Not really,' said Clopinet. 'The only thing is, my right leg is more tired than my left.'

'That's a mere nothing – you've no call to speak of it. Now, decide! What do you want to do? If Father were here, he would make me take you back, willy-nilly, to the tailor – and I'd have to do it! But Father isn't here. So, if you like, I'll take you to Trouville. It's not far and I can be home again before nightfall.'

'Oh, let's go to Trouville!' cried Clopinet. 'Dear François, you're saving my life! Since Mother isn't dying of grief, and since Father isn't grieving at all, I'll go to sea. After all, the sea has been kind to me – much kinder than some!'

In three hours they reached Trouville, which – in those far-off days – was just a poor fishing village. Here Uncle Laquille had a little house right on the shore, and a boat, and a wife, and seven children. He gave Clopinet a warm welcome. He listened to his story, praised him for not wanting to stoop to the mean trade of tailoring, exclaimed in admiration at his account of the night spent on the Great Cow, and swore by all the oaths of land and sea that the boy was clearly destined to great adventure. He promised that, the very next day, he would do his best to get him a place either in the Merchant Navy or in the Royal Navy.

'And in the meantime,' he said, turning to François, 'you must go home. Your father's a blockhead, so you'd best let him think the child is still with that master of his. Don't I know that tailor! He's a rogue – a real rogue! A skinflint too! Wickedly cruel with anyone weaker than himself; and a snivelling coward with anyone stronger! Why, I should be ashamed to think of any nephew of mine left in such hands!

'So be off with you now, François, and trust me to do what's best. Here's a boy that should bring honour to his family. For the time being, let them think he is at Dives. It will be at least two or three months before Left-hand-thread calls at your house again. When your father hears that the child has run away, that will be time enough to tell him that he's at sea. There, if he gets a beating sometimes, at least it will be from true men – from men of spirit – from *sailors*!'

François thought his uncle's plan a good one, and so did Clopinet. Before he left for home again, François gave Clopinet a bundle from his mother: clothing that she had patched up for him, something to wear on his feet, and a little money. To this last François added, out of his own pocket, two silver crown-pieces and a little bag of farthings as small change. Then he told Clopinet to be good, and hugged him and kissed him goodbye.

5

THE HOUSE ON THE SHORE

Uncle Laquille was a thoroughly good fellow: sweet-natured and gentle, as someone who had laboured and suffered and endured. Perhaps his worst fault was that his imagination too easily ran away with him. He had travelled all over the world and seen a great deal; and, in his reminiscences, everything appeared as extraordinary – dazzlingly beautiful, gigantic, hideous, or fantastically strange. When he had drunk a quantity of cider, he found it quite impossible to describe anything as it had actually been.

Clopinet listened eagerly to his tales, and asked him a thousand questions.

At supper-time, Aunt Laquille came in, and Clopinet met her for the first time. She was a large, gaunt woman dressed in a dirty old skirt and wearing on her head the cotton cap of a countrywoman of those parts. She had more of a beard than her husband, and seemed to have no idea that husbands were meant to be obeyed. It was quite clear that she did not welcome Clopinet in her house, and Uncle Laquille had hastily to explain to her that the boy would be with them only for a short time. She served his supper with a sour face, and remarked acidly, as she watched him eat, that he had the appetite of a sea-monster.

The next day Uncle Laquille set about carrying out his promises. He took Clopinet off to see the skippers of various craft. But all of them saw that the boy was lame, and refused to take him on. It was just the same when Uncle Laquille presented him for recruitment into the King's Navy.

Poor Clopinet, his hopes dashed, trailed back with his uncle to the little house on the sea-shore. There Uncle Laquille had to admit to his wife that they had failed: the boy's lameness had told against him. Moreover, since he had not grown up by the sea, he was without the bold front and easy, alert bearing of a born sailor.

'I could have told you that all along,' said Aunt Laquille. 'He's a good-for-nothing! He wouldn't do even for a clodhopper on his father's farm! You were a fool ever to take him on. You do nothing but idiotic things when I'm not there to stop you. Well, you must just take him on to the tailor or back to his family. I've enough children in this house as it is, without another one!'

'Have a little patience, wife!' Uncle Laquille pleaded. 'It's just possible that someone might want his help in cod-fishing.'

Aunt Laquille shrugged her shoulders. The village of Trouville already swarmed with children brought up to follow their fathers as fishermen. Nobody was likely to want this one, who had no experience and was of no particular concern to anybody.

Uncle Laquille still persevered on Clopinet's behalf. The next day he tried all over again, but in vain.

Everywhere there were more children than work for them to do.

Aunt Laquille now said that enough was enough. She had no intention of going on feeding an extra mouth in this way.

Uncle Laquille took Clopinet out sea-fishing with him. This was a great delight to the boy. He forgot his woes in the wonderful sensation of being rocked on these great waters that he loved so much.

When they went home, Uncle Laquille tackled his wife again: 'Whatever anyone says, he's a stout lad, all right! Afraid of nothing! Not seasick! Even got his sea-legs already! If only I could keep him with me, I'd make something of him, I swear!'

Aunt Laquille said nothing.

That night, when all the Laquille children had gone to bed, Clopinet could not sleep for the worries that went round and round in his head. Suddenly he heard the word 'tailor' spoken by his aunt. She was talking to her husband: 'My mind's made up! The tailor passes by here tomorrow morning on his way to Honfleur: you hand his apprentice over to him then. He'll know how to get sense into the boy. There's nothing like thrashing children till the blood runs – that teaches them manners!'

Uncle Laquille sighed deeply, but made no reply; and Clopinet knew that his fate was decided. His uncle could no more save him from the tailor than his own mother had been able to do.

He was determined to escape. He waited until everyone was asleep, and then he got up very quietly. He dressed himself, took up his bundle, which he had been using as a pillow, checked that his money was in his pocket, and made ready to leave his bedchamber.

A very strange bedchamber it was! There were only two sleeping-places – more bunks than beds – in the house; and these were occupied by the Laquille children and their parents, all squashed up together. So an armful of dried sea-weed had been put down as a mattress for Clopinet in a little upper cupboard that gave on to a dormer window. This cupboard was so high up that it could be reached only by means of a ladder from the room below. Now Clopinet put a foot out into the darkness to find the first rung of that ladder; but it wasn't there. Then he remembered that Aunt Laquille had taken the ladder away earlier in order to climb up to her loft at the other end of the room.

Clopinet lifted the rag of cloth that served as a curtain to his window, and saw that the night outside was clear, with a bright moon. By that light shining in through the window, he could see that the ladder he needed was indeed far beyond his reach; and it would be impossible to jump down from his cupboard into the room below without breaking his neck.

Oddly enough, the idea of those wings of his never occurred to Clopinet. His brother had teased him so much about them that he had not dared to mention them again. Even to himself he had begun to say that perhaps they were just part of a dream.

All the same, in one way or another, he had to get away; and he could not afford to wait for daylight, either.

He opened the dormer window to make sure that he would be able to squeeze through it. Yes; but when he stuck his head out, he saw that again the distance to the ground below was too great for him to jump.

The sea was still far away. The evening before he had noticed that the incoming tide washed against the piles on which the little house was built. But when would the tide be back again? He had been told that it was high tide twice every twenty-three hours; but Clopinet's arithmetic was not good enough for him to calculate from that.

'Well,' he said to himself, 'if the sea comes looking for me, I'll certainly jump down into it. I'm not afraid of the sea. The sea's my friend.'

His mind dwelt on this plan for a long time, and all the while he was at the ready, bundle in hand. Sometimes he dozed off in spite of himself, and in his dreams he was rocking on the sea in his uncle's fishing boat.

Suddenly a violent gust of wind blew open his window, which he could not have fastened properly. At once he was wide awake, and he was in time to hear those child-like voices he had heard before. They were passing his open window, going out to sea. This time he seemed to understand the meaning of their cries: 'Away! Away!' they were calling. 'To the sea—to the sea! Leave sleeping, and join us! Open wide your wings and come with us! To the sea!'

Clopinet felt his heart beat fast: his wings were opening! He sprang out of the window on to an old ship's mast which jutted from the Laquilles' house as a perch for their pigeons. He slid along this mast – or he flew, to his own way of thinking – and then dropped down into his uncle's boat. His uncle's boat was riding on the incoming tide!

The boat was securely moored with anchor and chain, so there was no way in which Clopinet could make use of it. But, anyway, the sea as yet was lapping only shallowly round the boat and up the shore.

Clopinet left the boat. Perhaps he swam, as sea-birds do; or perhaps he was carried along by the wind; or perhaps – but, whichever way it was, he was still dry as a bone when he landed on the open sands, among the sea-grasses.

Walking over that soft surface was difficult, and slow. But Clopinet persevered, struggling on and on, until tiredness overcame him. He laid himself down on the fine, warm sand, and instantly fell asleep.

He woke at sunrise, refreshed and, above all, happy to be free. His joy was soon overclouded, however. He had thought he was walking – or flying – towards Honfleur, whose light-house he had surely seen ahead of him. But, all the time, he had been mistaken: he looked about him and recognized his surroundings with a sinking heart. He had come this way two days before with his brother François. He had come this way from the direction of Villers and the Black Cows.

He was going back!

He considered. By this route the tailor would be coming from Dives, and he ran the risk of meeting him. Yet returning to Trouville was not to be thought of. Someone there might well see him and recognize him, and later put his enemy upon his track.

Clopinet decided to go on, following the line of the dunes, but keeping well away from the coast-road. He would stay by the edge of the sea, as far as possible. For he remembered his uncle saying that the tailor disliked the sea – rather, he had a horror of it. Old Left-hand-thread had never set foot in a boat without feeling that he would die of sea-sickness. The mere sight of a wave turned his stomach. When he had to travel along the coast, he never went by the shore. He used the path well above sea-level, and as far as possible from the sea itself.

So, following the sea's edge, Clopinet came to Villers. Here he kept a sharp look-out for anyone he knew, while he bought himself a loaf of bread. Then he hurried on, still keeping between the dunes and the sea, towards the Black Cows. When he reached them, and found himself once more in that remote, desolate spot, he felt the pure joy of a homecoming.

He had given up all idea of going back to his family. What his brother had told him made him realize that his father would never relent towards him; and his mother would never be able to protect him from his father.

He munched his bread while he gazed along the coast. Even the few days he had spent with his uncle had taught him a little of the geography of these parts. On a clear day, as this was, he could see that the mouth of the River Seine was a long way away, and that to reach Honfleur he would have to cross a countryside that was flat and almost without cover for a fugitive. The dunes and cliffs here, near the Black Cows, were his only hope. He could take refuge here, hide, and live alone.

He would have to live alone. The poor child went in fear of all the world by now. Aunt Laquille had by no means increased his trust in the human race. And he was not unused to solitude: his work so far had been the tending of his father's cows in a countryside with few passers-by. Above all, ever since his experience of the flying spirit-voices, he had had no fear at all of life in the wilds.

When Clopinet had worked all this out in his mind, he resolved to search out a hiding-place on the seaward side of the cliffs and dunes. There he would settle and live in safety, for always.

For always! So said Clopinet. He did not look ahead, even a little way, to the coming of winter. He did not attempt to calculate how long his tiny store of money might last. He did not wonder how he could possibly manage for food in such a place. For nothing grew there but sea-grasses that even sheep and cattle would not have eaten. Of course, there was the sea itself with its endless shellfish; but anyone would soon weary of that diet, especially when there was nothing to drink but water not as sweet as it might have been.

Clopinet simply could not look into the future. He was not like a child who had mixed with other children at school, and learnt to read and write. He had never left home in his life; he had never before left his mother. She had always been there, to set his bacon-soup down on the table before him, to tuck him up at night . . .

Now he was to be alone, *for always*. He tried to

imagine what that future might hold for him; but he could not.

Alone, *for always*. He repeated the words to himself, over and over again, and realized that he didn't really understand them at all. All he understood about the life ahead was this: *he must escape the tailor.*

6

THE HIDE–AWAY

Clopinet plunged among the rifts and eroded valleys of the dune.

At this point, near the Black Cows, the dune was more than a hundred metres high in some places, and cut steeply like cliffs. Its appearance was very beautiful and yet sombre too, with sheer walls mottled red, grey and an olive green stained with brown. They had the misleading look of solid rock.

On those heights Clopinet would dearly have liked to make his home, his eyrie; but how was he ever to get up there? Perhaps a way could be found . . .

He began by scrambling about on the lower slopes of the dune, where such climbing was possible. He found this less alarming than he had feared. He soon learnt where to expect a firm foothold; and he discovered that he could safely climb even the crumbling slopes if he kept to those parts where certain kinds of sea-plants grew. Equally, he learnt on what terrains not to trust himself.

In the end he managed to work his way right up into the heart of the dune. Here any movement of the marl seemed to have been a long, long time ago. Fissures and slopes were grass-grown, and he was able to move about freely without fear of slipping on unstable surfaces. He roamed more and more widely over what had once been rockfall and landslide, now more or less solid ground.

He came to a rocky, cliff-like part of the great dune, where he suddenly found himself gazing into a kind of grotto, or cave. It was partly a natural formation in the recess of a crag, and partly man-made, with brickwork. He went in, and found the place to be like a little dwelling hollowed out for human habitation. There was a stone bench; and a corner of the cave-house was blackened, as if fires had once been lit there. But no one could have lived there for a very long time: the fine turf at the entrance bore no trace of human tread; and brush-wood hung down thickly over the entrance – no one bothered any more to cut it back.

Delightedly Clopinet took possession of this abode, as tiny and remote as a hermit's cell. It appeared to have been abandoned many years before, probably because of the danger from landslides round about.

He set his bundle down inside, and then went to cut some dried grass to make himself a bed on the stone bench. As he worked, he reflected with satisfaction: 'Neither the tailor nor Aunt Laquille will ever find me here. I'm well off here; and if I had the company even of one of our cows, I should be really happy.'

He had never been very fond of his cows, but they had been company of a sort. Now he had none; and a sadness crept over him. He decided that this was the time to sleep, for he had enough bread to last for two days, and he meant to keep quite out of sight as long as there was any danger of the tailor being in the neigh-bourhood.

He slept deeply and long, right into the evening. Then he woke, rested and refreshed. The dusk of evening made him bold to venture out and explore his domain. He went all over what he was henceforth to call his garden. There were flowers growing in it; but otherwise it was an odd garden indeed. It was like a very deep ditch, thick with greenery, and with its walls on either side so near the vertical that he could see only a streak of sky overhead. It was rather like being at the bottom of a well; but this well was high up on the dune and there seemed to be no path by which one could climb up to it or down from it. Clopinet found that he could not remember how he had got here in the first place, and began to wonder if he would ever find the way out.

Now that he was no longer distracted by hunger or tiredness, he could begin to reason calmly and clearly about his present situation and the immediate future. He told himself that some other human being had once lived here, and therefore it was just not possible to be completely lost. He must still be quite near the sea, because he had kept to the seaward side of the dune, far from the path that went roughly along the middle – the very path along which he had escaped from the tailor.

But, if all this were so, why could he no longer see the sea?

He looked to right and left along the deep ditch, or ravine, where he now was. To the right, the ravine made a bend, so that he could not see far along it. To the left, the way was clear, and there was something like a natural pathway.

He followed the pathway to the left, and soon reached a section of wall, clearly man-made. The wall was pierced by a spy-hole, through which he looked. Now he saw the sea again, a hundred feet below him, and he saw the moon rising through thick black clouds.

The view was exactly to his liking. Here again was his friend the sea, whose voice came more clearly to him as the tide advanced. It would sing him to sleep more sweetly than when he had lain on the Great Cow.

He examined carefully the outside wall of the cliff – for at this point the dune was solid enough to form a real cliff, almost perpendicular and certainly unclimbable. Whoever had lived here long ago must have had good reason for hiding himself away so well: even his look-out was precipitously sited in this desolate spot.

Clopinet retraced his steps, meaning now to go to the other end of his curving ravine. But he was soon halted by a deep gash in the ground and a vertical wall of rock.

Next, by such light as the moon gave, he tried to find the way by which he must have come to this strange hide-away. he groped about in several fissures, but all of them proved to be closed off by landslides. The danger of further slides decided him to give up his attempts for the present, and to wait until daylight to search for a way out.

The moon was now clouding over, although the strip of sky that he could see directly above his head was still clear. He made the most of what light there was to get back into his cave-house, for his wilderness of a garden

was very uneven underfoot, and that made walking difficult.

He was no longer at all sleepy, and there was nothing to see or do: he began to feel depressed again. He longed for those little winged spirits to come and bear him company; but he could hear nothing above the sound of the wind. A storm was brewing, and already the dull roar of its voice drowned the voice of the sea.

At last Clopinet dozed off; but this time he slept only lightly, and started awake at any unusual noise.

Always in the past he had slept soundly and dreamlessly. Or if he did dream, he had had no recollection of his dreams on waking. But tonight he dreamed, and he knew he dreamed. He was lost among the dunes again, and he could not – he *could not* – find his way home. Then suddenly, lo and behold! he was back at home, and he heard his father's voice counting money, repeating over and over again the same number: 'Eighteen! Eighteen! 'Teen! 'Teen!' His father had been haggling over the amount of money to be paid to the tailor for the first year of Clopinet's apprenticeship. 'Eighteen! Eighteen!' Farmer Doucy insisted doggedly; while the tailor demanded 'Twenty!' But the farmer dug his heels in with his endless *eighteen*, until at last old Left-hand-thread gave way. The bargain was struck.

Then Clopinet seemed actually to feel the terrible claw-like hand of the tailor upon him. He gave a great cry – and woke up.

Where was he? The night was black as pitch inside his hide-away. But almost at once he remembered where he was, and why; and that calmed him. Only for a moment, however; for then, wide awake as he was, he heard with appalling distinctness a voice, only two paces from him, that gabbled over and over again: 'Eighteen! 'Teen! 'Teen!'

At the sound, Clopinet broke into a cold sweat all over his body. This was not the strong, forthright voice of his father – no, this had a shrill, cracked sound, just like the voice of the tailor when he had at last cried: 'Eighteen! Eighteen! 'Teen it is! Done!'

The tailor was here then! He had discovered his apprentice's hiding-place – he had come to carry him off! In panic Clopinet sprang up from his rocky bed. As he did so, something – or somebody? – whirled noisily round him and then fled from the cave, repeating: 'Eighteen! 'Teen!' The shrill voice faded into the distance.

So perhaps the tailor had only happened to come there to take shelter from the storm? And in the dark, he had not, after all, seen Clopinet as he slept. Then, when the boy woke and moved, the tailor had taken fright and fled. That must be the explanation. The idea that the tailor was a coward, more fearful even than Clopinet himself, had a wonderfully fortifying effect. Clopinet went back to bed again, this time with his stick by his side. He was resolved now to hit hard if his enemy should return.

He dozed off again, and then woke again. The storm had passed. Moonlight shone on the grass that grew at the entrance to his cave-house. It had been raining, and the leafiness that hung over the entrance shone in points like green diamonds. The night was still; and in

that stillness Clopinet was amazed to hear the deep
bellowing of a bull, then the bleating of goats and the
barking of dogs, all not far away. He listened, and the
sounds came again and again — so often that, if he shut
his eyes, he could imagine that he was at home and
hearing the farmanimals.

Yet he was in this cave-house in the wilds, far, far
from home. How could any farmstead and livestock be
so near?

At first the sounds, however strange in such a place,
were pleasant to him: they eased the terror of loneliness.
But then that 'Eighteen! 'Teen! 'Teen!' made itself heard
again, endlessly repeated by a number of voices coming
from all sides. He could imagine a whole gang of tailors
posted widely along the tops of the dune, to threaten
him and jeer at him.

Clopinet could not possibly go to sleep again. He lay
rigid and motionless, waiting for the coming of daylight. He heard no more voices.

As soon as it was light, he left his cave-house. He
looked well all around him, but saw nobody. A great
number of sea-birds and shore-birds, which must have
been sleeping on the heights of the dune, were now
passing overhead. He saw lapwings with their emerald-
green plumage, gambolling in the air with a thousand
graceful twists and turns; godwits, too; and a great
bittern, mournful bird, which passed overhead with its
neck pulled back to rest almost on its spine, and its feet
trailing out behind it. Clopinet knew none of these
birds by name. Indeed, he had never even seen them
close to before now, since there had been neither pond

nor river in his part of the countryside, and since migrant birds did not normally land there. He took pleasure in watching the birds now; but he was still puzzled and disturbed to remember the strange sounds of the night.

He resolved to find out if there was, after all, some human habitation – some farmstead – in the near neighbourhood.

Before that, he had to discover a way out from his hiding-place. But, by daylight, nothing could be easier. The way was narrow and choked with thorny under-growth; but there it was. He carefully noted its exact position, so that he should not miss it again, even at night. Then he proceeded to climb up to a good vantage point, whence he could survey the countryside round about.

As far as the eye could see, there was nothing but the wild, empty coastland. No sign of cultivation. Not the slightest trace of human habitation.

He began to think that goblins of darkness had been trying to frighten him. His brother, François, had said: 'There aren't such things as sea-spirits. There may be spirits on land, but that's another matter . . .' Clopinet's family believed in all kinds of spirits and fairy-folk, both good and bad: they believed them to be responsible for the sickness or health of their farmanimals. Who was Clopinet to set himself up as knowing better than his family? He himself had had no experience of spirits, before spending the night in the open, on the Black Cow; but from that time he had believed in sea-spirits. And if he believed in sea-spirits, he could surely believe in land-spirits.

He worried about such spirits, for now he had every reason to think them ill-disposed towards himself. Perhaps they wanted to prevent his settling on the cliff. Perhaps the tailor really was a sorcerer, with the power of coming magically in the night to torment him . . .

Such possibilities whirled foggily round and round in Clopinet's head; but of some things, at least, he was sure. The spirit that had cried *eighteen* had fled before him; and the other ones had not even dared to appear. They had contented themselves with mimicking the voices of creatures that he knew well already. Perhaps they had hoped to tempt him out of his safe refuge and then lead him astray in the darkness.

'Well,' he thought, 'another time they can make what row they please, I shan't budge. And I shan't lose myself again on the dune, because now I've really got to know it. And if those goblins dare to come into my cave-house again, I shall thump them for it.

'What my uncle said is true: I shall grow wings of courage.'

7

THREE FEATHERS

He started to look for drinking-water.

There was no shortage of water, for it came out all over the place. He noticed that the higher he climbed, the sweeter it was. Yet the water had always an earthy taste, which was unpleasant. At last he found water that trickled from rock and smelt of wild thyme; but this good water fell only drop by drop, grudgingly.

He needed a vessel of some sort in which to catch the drops.

Already he had noticed large fossilized oyster-shells stuck in the marl in various places. Almost all of them seemed broken. But now he searched thoroughly and found several which were both large and whole. He arranged these together, very carefully, one above the other, and the topmost one directly below the trickling drops of water. When the topmost shell was full of water, it overflowed into the one below, and so on. The shells were always full to overflowing; and thus he provided himself with a water supply always ready and always renewed.

He waited until he could carry one well-filled shell off with him into his garden, to drink with his meal. He had only dry bread to eat; but then, he had never been used to jam, and he did very well without it.

He did not find the day too long. The weather was fine, and he spent some time examining all the different plants which grew in the greensward outside his cave-house. They were quite unlike the plants of the open pasture-lands he had known. Some of them were very unattractive, all thorny or ready to sting him; but he did not mind that. Such plants seemed to him like guards at the ready to defend him against unwelcome visitors. Other plants delighted him by their beauty, and he was careful not to trample them underfoot. They brightened the surroundings of his hermitage, and it would have been wicked, he thought, to have harmed them in any way.

He spent a good deal of the day at his window, as he called the hole that pierced the old wall at the side of

the cliff. He satisfied his longing to gaze on the sea: he found it ever more beautiful. He watched the different boats far out at sea: none came in near the Black Cows, for the place was reputed dangerous.

The coast itself seemed deserted; there was not a soul to be seen. The emptiness emboldened Clopinet. Towards evening he ventured out on to the beach to gather shellfish for his supper; and then he looked carefully to see whether his window was visible from below. It was not: it was too high up, too small, and the wall itself was too well covered by vegetation. His eyes sought for the window in vain.

That night he slept like a top. He had walked so much and climbed about so much, in order to explore all the nooks and crannies of his wilderness, that he had no need to be lulled to sleep. His own weariness was enough. If the goblins amused themselves with talking and shouting, as on the evening before, he did not hear them.

The third day was occupied in exploring the base of the dune, to find a good hiding-place there in case he was surprised out on the open beach. He found not one good hiding-place, but a dozen. So, having planned for his safety in the future, he felt as free as a little wild animal that knows its own territory and its burrow.

He also remembered to get in a stock of shellfish, enough for one or two meals in his cave-house. Thus he would not need to be constantly going down to the shore.

There were plenty of sea-rushes growing along this coast, also broom, low willow, and other shrubs with pliable twigs and branches. He gathered suitable stems and took them home – already he called it *home*. There he used them to make himself a handsome basket, big and strong enough for most purposes.

He also made a good bed for himself from the seaweed that the sea had brought up on to the shore, and that had dried there.

Last of all, he became a hunter. He had always been a good shot with a stone. Now, having lain in wait for a long time, he managed to knock down a sea-partridge that he saw running and playing on the shore. It was a handsome bird, very plump; and the next step was to cook it. There was no problem in lighting a fire. Clopinet carried a tinder-box and steel in his bundle – things that no traveller was without in those days. Using also a flint, he had a flame going very soon, and fed it with dry leaves and brushwood. On this fire he suc- ceeded in cooking his bird. I don't say the meat was very good or without a certain smoky taste to it, but Clopinet found it excellent. He was only sorry that he could not offer a wing to his mother and a drumstick to his brother François.

This sea-partridge was not really a partridge at all, but rather like a swallow in appearance; and it lived off shellfish, not grain. It was indeed a handsome bird, with beak and neck-feathers a little like those of a partridge. In size it was only as big as a blackbird; so you can see that Clopinet was in no danger of indigestion from eating too much.

In the course of his hunting he saw many other birds which tempted him: sandpipers; plovers; sea-larks –

which, in fact, are not larks at all, but another kind of
wader; oyster-catchers, or sea-magpies; mergansers;
turnstones; sea-gulls; divers; and a great number of other
birds which he did not know. At the approach of
evening they came to frolic about on the sands, making
a great clamour. He noticed some very large birds that
swam about on the open sea at sunset, going further and
further out, as if they were in the habit of sleeping far
out at sea. Others came back to land and slipped into
the clefts of the dune.

There were some birds that, in the morning, flew up
to a great height and seemed to disappear into the little
white clouds that floated like waves high in the rosy sky.
It seemed as if these birds came down again only in the
evening, to take their supper on the rocks and sands.
Clopinet thought at first that they spent the day up in
the sky; but then he saw a very big one perched on the
highest point of the dune. Thence it came down,
wheeling about on the air-currents as it came – down
to its fishing-station. After that, there came another bird,
and another. Each bird left from the very top of the
dune and executed the same wheeling and downward
movement. Clopinet counted a score of them. He came
to the conclusion that the birds nested on the heights
and that they were really nocturnal, like owls.

Through his spy-hole of a window, Clopinet could
keep an eye on everything, watching the birds from
quite close, without himself being seen. He observed
something which interested him greatly. The sea-
swallows, who were describing wide circles round him,
very often let something fall from their beaks – perhaps

a little fish, or shellfish of some kind. At the same time, they swayed to and fro in the air, uttering a peculiar cry. It seemed to him that they dropped whatever it was on purpose, and gave warning of it by their cry. With his eyes he followed the actions of one bird in particular, and looked downwards when the object fell from its beak. He saw a movement on the ground: a brood of chicks were coming to get the food that their mother had let fall from far above. When he went down to the shore, he found that he had not been mistaken: the chicks were there. But when he tried to get near them to catch them – for they were too young to fly – the mother sea-swallow uttered another kind of warning cry. This made them scuttle from the open beach to the cover of the dune. Clopinet searched for them and found them crouched, motionless, underneath the vegetation there. He did not take any of the chicks, for fear of causing distress to the mother. She probably knew how many she had.

He watched how the various birds set about their fishing, and, in so doing, he learnt to fish himself. On most of the shore there were only shellfish to be had; but on the wet sands, when the incoming waves had retreated for a moment, great numbers of tiny fish lay stranded, very pretty and tasty-looking. Clopinet had only to be on the spot at that right moment to gather them up before the tide came to carry them away again.

He saw how deft and clever the fishing birds were. He copied them. He did not fear the sea now, but he was still wary of its violence and strength. He knew that he no longer had wings to carry him over the waves; it was no longer enough for him just to fancy he was a bird in order to become one. That strange power was only for times of great danger or despair; and he was far from eager to face such situations again. He preferred to learn to swim in the ordinary way. As he felt reasonable confidence in the water, within a day he was swimming like a sea-gull, without even knowing how he did it. Perhaps man has the power to swim, like all other animals, and only fear prevents him.

Yet the birds could swim for much longer than he without tiring; and they could see better underwater. It was not surprising that he caught fewer fish than they did. All the same, he found sand-eels everywhere. The sand-eel is a little fish, excellent to eat, which abounds on this coast. He caught and cooked some for his supper. If only he had had bread, he would have feasted like a king; but his stock was finished, and he dared not yet venture out to buy more in Villers.

He determined to do without bread for as long as he could.

Now he took it into his head to go looking for eggs, as this was the nesting season. Clopinet did not know that most sea-birds do not make nests, but lay eggs in the open, or almost in the open, on the sand or among the rocks. He found eggs just by good luck, when he was not even looking; but they were too small to be of much use to him. The big birds, which must lay big eggs, probably did so on the heights of the cliff, where it seemed impossible to climb. It was true that, on the side facing Clopinet's own wild territory, the cliff was only half as high as on the seaward side; but even so it presented a very steep escarpment, with earth-surfaces obviously loose and treacherous. Just to look up at it from below made Clopinet's head swim.

But every day found Clopinet less fearful. He learnt prudence – that is to say, to keep his head when faced with dangers, and to weigh up those dangers instead of blindly running away from them. Now he settled down to studying the contours and winding crevices of the great cliff, to such purpose that, in the end, he was able to climb almost to the summit without accident.

He was well repaid for his trouble, for almost at once he found four handsome green eggs. He put them into his basket, the bottom of which he had spread with seaweed. He also found some beautiful feathers lying about, and he gathered up three, which he stuck into his cap. They were long, slender and delicate-looking, white as snow. They must surely have come from the head or from the tail of the same bird.

As the eggs were still quite warm, he thought that the mother-birds must be here during the night to lay their eggs or to brood them: he could lie in wait and take the birds by surprise, and catch some. But then he reflected that, for one or two birds taken in this way, he would frighten off all the others, and run the risk of their deserting this nesting-site altogether. He decided that it was better just to take eggs when he wanted them, and leave the birds to themselves.

A week passed, and Clopinet had seen nobody on the shore or on the dune. He had been too busy to be bored. But now he had settled himself in comfortably and was pretty certain of his food supply; now the dune

and the shore had no parts that he had not explored and poked about in. And he began to find the days long and hardly knew what to do with his leisure.

Already he was more or less familiar with the habits of the wild creatures among whom he lived. He would have liked to have gone on to learn their names and the parts of the world they came from. He would have liked to tell somebody all that he had learnt. In short, he wanted someone to talk to.

The weather was very hot for May; the mud at the base of the dune was drying rapidly in the sunshine; and, at low tide, the way along the shore was becoming much easier. Clopinet occasionally saw people walking there; and then his heart beat fast with the longing to speak to them, if only to say: 'What a lovely day to be out walking!' He never dared accost anyone, however: if anyone should ask him who he was and what he was doing there, what could he reply? He knew that people disapproved of vagrants; sometimes they were rounded up and clapped into prison. He was too straightforward by nature to invent for himself a false name and a false history. He would much rather not show himself at all.

One morning, however, the wind from the east brought to him the sound of church bells. It was Sunday. From force of habit he spruced himself up. He washed, and he combed his hair as best he could; he put something on his feet; and he stuck the three white feathers into his cap. Then he started off walking, hardly knowing where exactly he was bound. He was in the habit of going to Mass on Sunday. At home it was a day for meeting and talking with the other young lads of the parish, his relations or friends. They would play at skittles; sometimes they danced. So the ringing of the church bell was a summons to social life for Clopinet: he simply could not conceive of being alone on a Sunday.

And who knows – he might meet his brother François, again! He would have risked a good deal for news of his family; and he determined to take a risk. After all, the tailor should be a long way from the neighbourhood by now.

Going straight as a bird in flight, Clopinet cut across the empty coastland, and soon found himself approaching Villers. As he knew nobody there, and nobody knew him, he hoped to pass unnoticed. But at least he would look upon other Christian faces and hear again the sound of the human voice; and no one would pay any special attention to him. That was what had happened before, on his previous visit.

But this time he was very much surprised to see that people were all staring at him, and even turned round to follow him with their eyes.

8

THE TAILOR AGAIN

Clopinet was worried by the attention he was attracting so strangely in Villers. He thought of leaving the place at once. But then, as he was passing a baker's shop, the craving for bread overwhelmed him. He stopped in the doorway to ask for some.

'And how much do you want, my little lad?' asked the baker. He spoke almost too jovially, and he was staring at Clopinet in an odd way.

Clopinet wanted enough bread to last him for several days. He said: 'Can you give me a really big loaf?'

'By all means!' said the baker. 'You can have two loaves, if you like; or three, if you can carry them.'

'I'll take three,' said Clopinet. 'I can easily manage that.'

'I expect there are a good many of you at home, to need so much bread?' the baker remarked slyly.

'Well . . . So it would seem . . .' Clopinet did not like to lie.

'Oh ho! We keep ourselves to ourselves, do we? Too proud to chat, eh? Won't you just say who you are and where you live – for I don't know your face at all, and you're not from these parts, I think?'

'No, I'm not from these parts,' said Clopinet. 'But I

really haven't time to stay and chat. Please, give me my three loaves and tell me how much money I owe you.'

'Well, now,' said the baker, 'I'm afraid your bread will cost a good deal. You see, bread's very dear in our part of the country. But I tell you what! Give me the three feathers from your cap, and you can come back here every Sunday for a month and take away as much bread as today, without paying out any money for it at all. That's a fair offer, and you'd do well to take it.'

At first Clopinet thought the baker was making fun of him. But, as the man persisted, Clopinet realized with sudden shrewdness that his three feathers must be something very special. The feathers were what people had been staring at, not him! He took them out of his cap, and the baker already had his hand out to take them, when Clopinet paused. His three feathers looked so very beautiful, and he had climbed so high to find them, at peril of his life. As for money, with the two silver crowns he already had, he felt rich for the rest of his life.

Clopinet drew back his hand.

'No,' he said. And then: 'Here's money. Pay yourself from that for your three loaves. I'll keep my feathers.'

'Well then, would you like bread twice a week instead of once?'

'No, thank you. I'd rather pay with money.'

'Or four loaves a week for two months?'

'I've told you: No!' said Clopinet. 'I'm keeping my feathers.'

The baker gave him his three loaves, and Clopinet paid him, and went off. To reach the road which would

take him homeward, he had to turn the corner at the
baker's shop and follow the street almost back upon
itself. So, for a moment, he found himself directly
behind the bakery, and he could hear the baker talking
to his wife. 'No!' he was saying. 'He wouldn't give me
his feathers, not for forty-eight pounds of bread!'

Clopinet stopped underneath the window to listen. A
woman's voice replied: 'Were they really feathers from a
hernshaw?'

'Oh, they were genuine all right! And the hand-
somest I've ever seen!'

'Devil take the boy, then,' said the woman. 'Those
feathers are so hard to find nowadays, since the hernshaws have stopped nesting along the coast. You can get
as much as a gold louis for one plume! That little lot

would have been worth three louis to us! Well, you'll just have to run after the child and offer him cash down for his feathers. Perhaps, after all, he'd rather have cash than a credit of bread.'

Clopinet, as has been said, did not care about money. He set off again with quickened pace; and, while the baker was looking in one direction, he escaped in another, and so made his way back towards the dune.

This incident made him think. He asked himself why the feathers of this hernshaw should be so valuable. How was it possible for a bird's feathers to be worth a golden louis each? 'I should have thought a feather was just something you could play with or stick in your cap, a knick-knack, a something-and-nothing. But goodness! if I'd asked the baker to feed me for a whole year, he would probably have agreed, just to get his hands on my three feathers!'

Clopinet was experiencing the pleasure of owning something which was a great rarity, something perhaps of unguessed, marvellous virtue. And he could afford to disregard money-value, since money was not of much importance in his present way of life.

Preoccupied with his thoughts, he was following the main path through the middle of the dune, without any idea of possible danger. Suddenly he became aware of a voice behind him, still very distant, but so shrill and piercing that the words reached him quite clearly. 'You say he must have gone this way?' the voice almost screamed. 'Don't worry – I'll catch him! And if he doesn't fancy selling his feathers, all the better: I'll take them from him by force. Then we shall have them for nothing, and that's the best way of doing business!'

It was a voice never to be forgotten: the tailor was after him! Instantly Clopinet's wings of fear carried him right off the road and into the bushes at the side of it.

Once there, he felt ashamed of his own cowardice – he who had climbed the great dune and swum in the sea, two things that Left-hand-thread would never have dared attempt. Clopinet thought to himself: 'I must be a man, and stop being afraid of another man. Otherwise, all my life I shall be a wretched creature, never free to go my own way. After all, I'm as big and as strong as that horrible little tailor; and Uncle Laquille told me for a fact that he's brave only with those who are not. So come on, let's deal with him once and for all! And may the good sea-spirits protect me!'

So saying, Clopinet stuck his three feathers jauntily back into his cap. Then he laid his loaves down on the grass, and, gripping his stout stick, he returned to the path. He stood there boldly, right in the way the tailor would come, resolved to thump him so well that he would never trouble Clopinet again.

But when the tailor appeared – when Clopinet actually saw him, the boy's heart failed him. He wanted to run away again – he was on the point of doing so. But then he began to wave his arms about, thinking of them as his wings of courage, and at the same time he whirled his stick round most purposefully. He had taken his stand on a large stone at the side of the road, and he was ready to defend his treasure and his liberty.

The tailor stopped dead. He took two paces backwards, and said with a kind of surprised snigger

that was meant to be ingratiating: 'Well, I never did! It's my own little apprentice! Clopinet, my dear, don't you recognize me? I'm your friend and well-wisher.'

'Oh, yes?' answered Clopinet. 'So much so that you want to steal my feathers from me. I know!'

'What an idea!' cried the tailor, all astonishment. 'Whoever can have told you such a thing?'

'Oh, spirits of the air, I should think,' said Clopinet. At those words he saw Left-hand-thread blanch and tremble, for the tailor was a great believer in the supernatural. He recovered himself enough to say: 'Come now, child! You're being really naughty! You must tell me exactly where the hernshaws nest, that give you such feathers. I ask nothing more from you.'

Clopinet answered: 'They nest in a place so high that

only birds and spirits can reach it. That means that I'm not afraid of you – do you understand? If you try anything against me again, I shall carry you up to that high place as a hernshaw carries up a crab, and then I shall throw you down from there – down to the very bottom of the sea!'

So spoke Clopinet, carried away by a frenzy of fury and pride.

The tailor really believed that the boy must have sold himself to the Devil. Old Left-hand-thread muttered and mumbled and turned on his heel. He took the road back to Villers again as fast as he could go.

Clopinet was both astounded and delighted at his victory. He cut into the dune again to pick up his loaves, and then carried them nimbly back with him up to his cave-house, his home.

9

NIGHT HERONS

Back in his cave-house, Clopinet felt a great need to talk to someone; so he talked aloud to himself.

'Well, that's over and done with!' he said. 'I shall never be so afraid of anything again. No one's ever going to carry me off again where I don't want to go. I'm free of all that – free – free! And if some spirit of the sea gave me my courage, then it's a gift I mean never to lose!

'And now,' he went on to himself, 'I shall go looking for more feathers from that wonderful bird. When I have enough, I shall sell them for a great deal of money, and then I shall go back to my father and say: "There's no need for me to be a tailor. Lame I may be, but I can earn more money in a day than my brothers in a year." And my father will be satisfied with that, and let me live as I want.'

He was glad to be back in his solitude again. He was glad to have bread, and good bread, too. He feasted on nothing else that day. The fear of going hungry, or of having to spend his time fishing for every meal, had worried him. But now he knew he could go freely wherever he wanted, to buy whatever he needed. He thought beyond the catching of little birds and fish for his food. He wanted something more – the beautiful plumes that made the countrypeople wild with envy and the horrible tailor wild with rage.

The next day he did something difficult and dangerous. He did not wait for daylight, but climbed in the dark right up into the very midst of the great peaks carved out of the cliffs; and he climbed so nimbly and so quietly that he did not wake a single bird as he went.

He settled in a convenient spot to one side, where he could lie still, making no movement, but able to see everything.

He had not ventured as far as this on his first visit, and he was surprised now to find a ruin he was unaware of until he knocked against it. In the old days, a look-out post had been set up here, from which semaphore signals could be sent out. The look-out men could see everything at sea, and pass any information on. This post had been part of a system for checking the theft and smuggling of salt, once very widespread.

The observation hut had collapsed with one side of the great cliff. Its burst planking and framework still remained partly standing, caught in a fissure. And Clopinet could see to what use the ruin was put now: the whole site had been taken over as a safe refuge by his marvellous birds, and they perched freely on the timbers.

The hernshaws had always liked trees, but, because of their valuable plumage, they had been hunted and harried in the woods and round the ponds elsewhere in the countryside. Only here had they been able at last to set up a colony secluded and safe: the ruined hut was invisible from outside and its very existence had been long forgotten.

A little marsh had formed at some distance from the old landslide, and many other water birds had made new homes here.

The observation post explained the existence of the cavehouse and the look-out window lower down. Almost certainly the look-out men, who were supposed to live in the more exposed, more dangerous observation hut, had hollowed out and built up the cave-house, without the knowledge of their superior officers. Here, secretly, they could come for better shelter in stormy weather.

From his short stay in Trouville, Clopinet had brought away a new shrewdness and forethought: he was glad to be in sole possession of the secret of his cave-house and of the nesting-site of the hernshaws.

He studied the hernshaws' nests, roughly built of branches wedged into the angles made by the wooden framework of the old hut. At first he saw only the females, sitting so calmly on their eggs; but soon the males began to arrive to rest after their night's hunting.

Because of the bird's nocturnal habit and also because of its cry, the old naturalists called it *nycticorax*, that is, night crow. But the birds are true herons; and they are rightly named night herons. When they have young to feed, however, they may hunt during the day as well as the night.

No young birds had hatched out as yet in this colony, and so the males came here to sleep.

Clopinet had seen the birds first of all from below, and he had thought them to be white. But now he realized that they were white only on their underside and neck. Their wings were a pearly grey; the back was mantled in a glossy greenish black; and from the crown of the head, which was of the same gloss, there swept down to the back those long and slender white plumes, usually three. Many of the birds did not have this plumage as yet, or had it no longer. A number of the precious feathers had been moulted and lay scattered over the rocks, to be blown here and there by the wind. In spite of the temptation, Clopinet made no move to collect any; he was more interested to observe the birds' behaviour. So far they had ignored him, as the males were attentive only to their females.

Gradually, however, they became aware of the presence of a stranger in their midst. The cry of one bird warned the others. They all turned their heads in his direction.

At first Clopinet was rather alarmed to see so many great red eyes looking at him. There must have been about fifty males, as big as young turkeys, and armed with long beaks and sharp claws. If they had all set upon the inquisitive boy, they could have done him a good deal of harm; but they only gazed at him as if in stupefaction. He made not the smallest movement, so they lost interest in him. They began to squabble among themselves, with wing-blows that did no injury. They scratched themselves; they stretched; they even yawned like people who are tired out. At last, each bird chose a convenient spot and went to sleep there, standing on one leg.

Clopinet got up quietly and gathered in his harvest of feathers without disturbing the birds. Then he climbed down the way he had come. He had wisely resolved to do nothing that might make the birds desert their site. He would not take any more eggs from the females.

He came back the following night before the males had returned from their hunting. He was careful not to wake the broody females, but put bread in front of their nests, thinking that they would like it and so take kindly to him. It was a child's plan, but it worked. Almost all birds like bread, however different it may seem from their usual diet; and the next morning Clopinet saw that his bread had been eaten. So he went on with his plan, and soon the night herons, male and female, became used to seeing him about. They did not trouble to move far away on his approach, and in the end did not move away at all. Young night herons hatched out which knew Clopinet before they learnt any fear of man. From the beginning they were so tame that they came to him freely, perched on his knees, and went to sleep there. They would eat bread from his hand, and followed him to the edge of the dune when he went away.

He took such pleasure in all this that he was never bored nowadays. He began to love these wild birds as he had never loved his pigeons and poultry at home. Looking back, he scorned such farmyard acquaintance-ships: now he was proud to have won the trust of wild creatures whose hidden sanctuary the countrypeople had searched for in vain.

He became fond of all the other birds, too. He scattered crumbs of bread everywhere he went. He made a practice of walking slowly and steadily, without too much noise. He never made any sudden, threatening movement that might frighten any of them. He was rewarded by seeing that he no longer put the birds to flight by his approach. Instead, they fluttered and frolicked in the air just above his head, or landed at his feet.

Now he reproached himself bitterly for the killing of the sea-partridge. He went off and bought himself cheese and meat, so that he should never again be tempted to kill one of these dear companions of his solitude.

He did not go to Villers to do his shopping. He was afraid of being recognized there and perhaps pestered and followed by the baker. He had noticed a hamlet that was nearer for him, for it lay on the coast towards the end of the dunes. This was the little village of Auberville; and here he found all that he wanted, even some of last season's apples, for which he paid dearly, of course. Sometimes he indulged himself with little extravagances. He treated himself to a jug of cider – he loved cider.

But he was careful never to display his white plumes, and not to hold unnecessary conversation with anyone. Henceforth, he had two secrets to keep. First, he must conceal his name and where he came from. He did not intend to be taken forcibly back to his family. Secondly, no one must know of his home on the great cliff. He did not want inquisitive children attracted there, or anyone on the look-out for hernshaw plumes.

Silent himself, Clopinet listened to the conversation of others; and, in so doing, he learnt a good deal about

the countryside and its wildlife. The young people of
the village knew many of the birds of the coast and their
habits. They spoke only of two kinds as being of special
value. There were the hernshaws, or night herons, which
could no longer be found: either they hid themselves
away too well or they had stopped nesting in those
parts. The other birds were the grebes: they were birds of
passage, and people had hunted them so much that they
had become very rare and shy. Clopinet asked questions
about the grebe, and learnt that the beautiful thick
plumage from its breast was sold to men in the feather-
trade, who came through Auberville twice a year. In the
end, all such plumage was used in fashion trimming.

As Clopinet already had a dozen of his white plumes,
he wanted very much to know the exact day and hour
when the dealers would be passing. He wanted to do
business with them. But he was wary of asking too
many questions, and so he simply promised himself that
he would find out more all in good time.

10

CLOPINET GOES HOME

Clopinet was rather surprised that no one was searching for the night herons where he himself had found them. But on this point he heard a piece of gossip which alarmed him. Somebody said that, at one time, the birds could indeed be found in the trees on the great cliff. But, since then, a huge section of cliff had fallen into the sea, and there were no trees left to retain the earth with their roots. So nobody ventured there now: it was believed that the weight of one human being would be enough to bring down the remainder of the cliff.

After that piece of information, Clopinet went home in some uneasiness of mind. After all, he lived on that very cliff and nearly every morning climbed to the top of it.

That night, he was afraid. The sea was up, and the sound of it reached him gustily on the wind. At every moment he would start from sleep, thinking that the sound was the cliff beginning to fall. He had examined the spot too closely not to realize that his hermit's cell was hollowed from exactly the same substance as the Black and White Cows. Those huge boulders on the shore had once been part of a cliff, and had fallen with it. The sea was continually eating into the base of the dunes and their cliffs. Every winter, people said, the greedy sea swallowed more. The big boulders which seemed to make Clopinet's refuge so secure could well be resting on ground as ready to crumble as the loose earth that covered it. Even supposing that the ground did not give way beneath him, still the ground above could fall, block his way out, and bury him alive in his cave-house.

He hardly slept at all for anxiety. He had been forced into thinking of the future, and that bred in him a thousand midnight fears. Fortunately, however, he was possessed of a passion stronger than any fear of danger: he absolutely must live free, and be his own master, in a state of Nature. He hardly knew the word 'Nature', but he was in love with the life of the wild. Proudly he resisted any temptation to return to the comparative ease of his father's farm and the cosiness of family life.

He stayed where he was, in his eyrie. He reasoned that the birds nested even higher than he. They had known the place for longer than any human being, and perhaps instinct told them that their heights were safe, at least for the time being.

All that summer he remained on the great cliff. He laid in his supplies by shopping now in one place, now in another, so that he did not become well known anywhere. He accustomed himself to living only on what he got from the sea or on wild fruits. He was determined not to be ruled by a demanding appetite. Little by little he became used to a diet so simple that no craving for delicacies could draw him away from his sea-shore.

He managed to waylay the feather-dealers on their rounds and to bargain with them, when there was no one else about. He made a deal with them. Wisely, he did not ask too much for his feathers, as he wanted to build up goodwill for the future. He satisfied himself with a silver crown-piece for every feather; and, as he had collected some fifty, that gave him twelve shining golden louis. This was an enormous sum of money for those days – much, much more than would ever normally have been earned by a little farm lad of his age.

When Clopinet found himself the possessor of such wealth, he decided to go home to his family. But before that he wanted to see his Uncle Laquille again, in Trouville.

During the summer his clothes had become very ragged and worn from his continual climbing about on the dune, and he had never done any mending. He wanted to appear before his family reasonably well-dressed; so, before starting for Trouville, he went to Dives. Here he ordered a brand-new outfit, some underlinen, and stout new shoes. He paid a good price for the lot; and then he was ready.

Just before the onset of winter, he set off for Trouville, stick in hand and money in pocket. As he walked into the village, he met his uncle, in tears, coming away from the church. He had just buried his wife, and – although Aunt Laquille had made his life a misery – the poor man was weeping for her as if she had been an angel.

Uncle Laquille was amazed to see Clopinet again. He had supposed him to be back with his family; and, anyway, he hardly recognized him – Clopinet had changed so much. He had grown; he was tanned by the sea winds; all his climbing and other energetic exercise had made him stronger, and he looked it. His weak leg had become as good as the other one, so that he no longer limped. Above all, the expression on his face had changed: he had an alert, keen look nowadays, and a confident and reliable air. His new clothes were better than anything Left-hand-thread ever made for his country customers; and his turn-out was altogether a great improvement.

Uncle Laquille was much struck by Clopinet's general appearance. 'And where've you come from?' he cried. 'Not from your family?'

'No,' said Clopinet. 'But quickly – tell me, how are they all? We can talk of my affairs afterwards.'

'I can't tell you any news,' his uncle answered. 'When you ran away from us that night – oh, it's nearly six months ago, I think – yes –'

'Yes, yes, uncle – I counted the moons.'

'Yes, well, I worried about you and I searched for you where I could. But about twelve days after you left, the tailor came by again and said that he had seen you in good health near Villers. He had not wanted to force you to go with him, because he supposed your family had charge of you again and had sent you there on some errand.

'After that, I stopped worrying about you.

'Then my poor wife fell ill, and I never left these parts again except to go to sea when I had to. So, you see, I know nothing of your family. Of course, they must think you've gone to sea: that was what you and François had agreed on. He will have told them so in the end and in all good faith.

'I think you can go home now without fear of being handed back to the tailor. I don't know what you said to him when you last met near Villers; but he swore that he'd rather take the Devil as apprentice than a madman as ferocious as you. I think you must have shown him your sharp teeth, and I don't blame you: he would have led you a dog's life.'

'I showed him my stout stick,' answered Clopinet. 'You foretold what would happen, uncle: I grew wings of courage.' And then he told the whole story, and brought out from his pocket all his money, to the amazement of his sailor-uncle.

'Well!' cried Uncle Laquille. 'So you're rich now, and you can lead whatever life you please! You're a useful lad for any skipper to take aboard; nobody would refuse to have you now. You can sail to faraway countries where the birds are quite different from your hernshaws, but just as rare and beautiful. There are the bosun-birds, the white egrets of America, the birds of Paradise, the phoenix that rise again from their ashes, the condors that carry off cattle, and a hundred others that you have no idea of.'

'It's true that I need to see more of the world,' said Clopinet. 'I know almost nothing; and I must learn.'

'You learn everything when you travel,' said Uncle Laquille grandly.

Uncle Laquille's words did not altogether convince his nephew. The sailor had gone right round the world

without ever having learnt to read a book; and Clopinet was beginning to see, from his tales, that he had wildly wrong ideas on the simplest of subjects. He believed that certain kinds of bird never ate at all, but lived on thin air. He believed that others never reproduced themselves in any normal way but were born from the barnacles on the below-water timbers of ships. Clopinet himself was quite ready to believe in spirit-birds – that is to say, in spirits taking on bird-forms and bird-voices. But he had already observed too much of the laws of Nature to be able to accept the mistakes and miscon- ceptions of his uncle.

The idea of travel, however, tempted him. To relieve the tedium of his solitude, he had often dreamed of voyages to far-off lands.

Now Uncle Laquille advised him to go to Honfleur and take passage on some ship for England. There were always some bound for that destination. In England the grebes nested, and there Clopinet could take as many as he wanted. But when the boy learnt that he must kill them and skin them to have their plumage, he shook his head. The idea filled him with horror.

After supper, Clopinet walked along the sea-shore with his uncle, and they talked again of his going to England, and to Scotland, too. Ahead of them, through the growing dusk, they could see the big boats, which were getting ready to leave the next day for Honfleur; and Clopinet's heart beat fast with excitement. His mind was almost made up: he would come to some arrangement with the skipper of one of the craft. Yes, he would go . . .

Then he heard the little childlike voices that he knew so well. They were passing overhead. 'They're here!' he cried. 'They've come to find me!'

His uncle had no idea what he meant. He stood openmouthed, waiting for some explanation. But Clopinet waited for nothing. He ran off at full tilt, with arms outspread like wings, following the flight of those invisible spirits which called ceaselessly to him.

At first the flying voices seemed to follow the shore in the direction of the embarkation quay. Then suddenly they swerved aside, left the sea altogether, and turned inland across country.

Clopinet rushed after them, following for as long as he possibly could, but never able to raise himself into the air as he went. At last he returned to his uncle, breathless and spent.

Uncle Laquille thought the boy must be out of his mind. 'What!' he cried. 'Do you really believe that curlews are spirits?'

'Curlews? What do you mean, uncle?'

'Don't you know the birds? It's true they travel only on dark nights, and that no one has ever seen them. People wouldn't know of their existence, if somebody didn't sometimes fire by chance into the middle of a flock, and bring one down. But that's only very, very rarely, for they say curlews fly faster than a shot from any gun. I do agree that they're extraordinary birds: they lay their eggs in the clouds, and the wind hatches them.'

'No, uncle!' Clopinet said sharply. 'If these really *are* birds – curlews, as you call them – then they certainly don't lay their eggs in the clouds. And if they are not birds – if they are spirit-voices, as I think they are – then they don't lay eggs at all. Their call may be like a curlew's – yes, that's possible. The first time I ever heard them, I said to myself: "Oh, those are night birds passing over!" But then I listened more carefully, *and I understood what they were saying.* They called to me; they made my wings of courage grow; they taught me to skim over the sea without getting wet, that night I spent on the Great Black Cow. They helped me to fly from your house, down from that little high window. They've always helped and comforted me. I believe in them; I love them; and wherever they tell me to go, I shall follow them.'

'And yet,' retorted his uncle, 'you didn't follow them just now?'

'They did not wish it. They left the sea-shore, and that meant that I must not go on board any boat tonight. They flew away in that direction, to the south. Tell me, isn't my own home in that direction?'

'Certainly it is. About ten miles from the sea, that's all.'

'Very well. That's the way I'll go tomorrow morning. I must go home to greet my parents and give them the money I've earned.'

'An excellent idea – except that they'll hang on to the money, and then you'll have none to travel with.'

'I can always go back to my hidey-hole in the cliff and gather a stock of feathers all over again. And by then I shall have Father's agreement to my going to sea.'

Clopinet followed his plan. He found out the road that he should take; and the very next day, towards noon, he was walking up to the gate of his father's home-paddock.

11

AT THE APOTHECARY'S

The first person Clopinet saw was his mother. She recognized him a long way off, in spite of his changed appearance; and when she had him in her arms again, she could have died for joy.

Clopinet was deeply moved. He had been gloomily imagining that she cared very little about him. Now he saw clearly that she truly loved him, all the more so because she had been compelled to let him go from her.

His father and his brother François, and all the others rushed up and gave him a great welcome. They saw how well-dressed he was, how healthy-looking – and his lameness was cured, too. To their way of thinking, all this proved plainly that he had suffered nothing by his travels – for they assumed that he had come from a great distance. François himself thought so: since parting from Clopinet, he had not seen Uncle Laquille, who could have told him otherwise.

Farmer Doucy welcomed his son, but, at the same time, he grumbled mildly at Clopinet for having gone against the wishes of his family in his choice of a livelihood. And, of course, he did not fail to add this: that if Clopinet did not manage properly to earn his own living, then he would be a burden on them all.

Clopinet took this meekly enough. He said: 'Father, I hope to go on earning an honest living, without harm to man or beast.' Then, without making a great fuss about it, he showed the contents of his purse to his father. 'Here's what I've been paid for six month's work. If you need the money, dear Father, or if you would even just like to have it, I beg you to take it all. Next year I should be able to bring more.'

All the family opened their eyes wide in amazement at the sight of Clopinet's gold; but Farmer Doucy shook his head. 'How did you come by that money, boy? You must explain yourself. I'm only a plain farmer, and I haven't gone roving round seas and to foreign cities, but even I know full well that an apprentice ship's boy, or any boy of your age, is lucky just to be earning his keep.'

Clopinet saw that his father suspected him of some wrong-doing, so he told him frankly where his money came from. Farmer Doucy accepted the explanation, for it was well known locally that certain kinds of bird-plumage were much sought after by dealers. He remarked only that hernshaws were no longer to be seen in that region: doubtless, he said, Clopinet had, in fact, found them much further away. Farmer Doucy continued obstinately to believe that his son must have spent the summer in travelling abroad.

That belief rather suited Clopinet. Only the day before he had refused to answer his uncle's questions about the *exact* spot on the coast where he had lived all that summer. With his family, equally, he now maintained a discreet silence. He knew that, if he mentioned the Black Cows and the great cliff, his parents would never let him return to such a dangerous place. So he allowed his family to go on thinking he had come from Scotland – he remembered the name of the country from his uncle's conversation – and that he had been wild-fowling there.

He was able fairly well to deal with the questions put to him on that first day at home. In his family, no one knew anything of foreign parts, so that he found it easy to satisfy their curiosity. He told them that in Scotland people ate bread, vegetables and meat, just as elsewhere; and that trees did not grow with their roots in the air. In short, there were no more marvels to be seen there than elsewhere.

'Well done!' his father said to Clopinet towards the end of family supper. 'What I like about you, boy, is that you don't tell fairy-tales and silly lies like your Uncle Laquille. Go on being so sensible, and you'll be all right. You've already been sharp enough to bring saleable goods back with you from abroad, and made a profit on them, too. No, I won't deprive you of your money; it's yours. But I'll buy land with it which can be your very own. That will be the founding of your fortune.'

Clopinet said: 'If you don't want any money for yourself, I'd rather use it to go on my travels. I might be lucky again.'

But what Uncle Laquille had foreseen happened. Farmer Doucy could not take seriously what his son said; and he could not imagine any better investment for money than in plots of grass and apple trees, with cows. Nor did he think it right for a mere child to have such a large sum to spend as he fancied. He praised

Clopinet for his good sense in bringing the money home; but, for all that, he believed the boy might squander it foolishly, if it were given back to him.

Clopinet had to yield, but he felt as if his wings were being clipped for him. He went sadly to bed that night, knowing that his travels were now postponed indefinitely. But he dreamed that his spirits spoke to him and said: 'Take heart! We shall never desert you. You have done as we wished, and we shall reward you well for it.'

So Clopinet resigned himself. He admitted to himself, too, that it was nice to sleep in a warm feather bed again. The last fortnight had been much colder on the coast, and he had not been so comfortable in his cave-house. Dampness had sweated from the walls, and the winds had rushed in; and he could protect himself properly from neither.

Life was pleasant, on the other hand, in the Doucy home. The Doucys were neither poor nor mean. There was always plenty of good bread and good cider; and Clopinet's mother was a positive genius at bacon soup. Clopinet was her favourite. She petted him and pampered him with a tenderness to which he could put up no resistance. He allowed himself to sink right back into family life, and came to the conclusion that he might as well spend the winter months at home. He saw flocks of migrant birds coming from the sea and taking their course inland, either to winter in the marshes, or to fly further still in search of warmer seas. He told himself that this was not the time of year to find nests in the north.

He had not wanted to tell more lies than necessary, so

he had simply assured his father that he had entered no agreement to go to sea again. He hoped to lead his parents gently towards giving him his full liberty. They must be prepared at last to see him depart without argument or bitterness.

He could not stay at home doing nothing, so he had to start herding and tending the cows again. That bored him terribly. The slow, heavy beasts were less and less to his liking; and the flat pasture-lands, with no view except of the sky, depressed him. In spirit, he was always on the wing over the sea and the cliffs.

One day his father sent him off to Dives to fetch some medicament from the apothecary there. The town was very ancient, but Clopinet was no antiquarian. He was interested only in the seaward side of the town, and, even there, he found the flat, sandy coastline wearisome to the eye. Then he came to the narrow fairway replacing the great port, from which, long ago, William the Conqueror's fleet had sailed for England. In this channel Clopinet saw some of the big boats which still did a little trade with Honfleur; and the longing to go at least so far was strong enough almost to make him forget his errand.

But he resisted his impulse, and asked the way to the apothecary's.

At the apothecary's he had to wait while the draught was being made up; and again he nearly forgot his errand in a sudden excitement. His attention was riveted by something in the apothecary's window: a ruff, otherwise known as a sea-peacock. The bird stood there motionless on its wooden perch. Clopinet was enraptured. The apothecary noticed the boy's wonder, and was amused by it. He took the bird – which really seemed alive, for its eyes shone and its beak was open – and let Clopinet handle it. It was stuffed. Clopinet had never conceived of such a thing, and had to have the process explained to him.

Then he spoke with an eagerness and decisiveness which, from a boy seemingly so simple, took the apothecary by surprise. He asked if the man would be willing to teach him how to preserve and stuff in just the same way.

'Well,' answered the apothecary, 'if you really want to help with the job, I'd be delighted. Always provided you turn out to have as much skill as you seem to have determination!'

Then he told Clopinet that the Curé – the parish priest – and the nobleman at the great house, a Baron, were both keen amateur ornithologists. (For the first time Clopinet heard of *ornithology* – the knowledge of birds and their classification in families, genera and species.) These two men secured as many different specimens as they could: the Baron of Platecôte regardless of cost, the Curé at the cost of whatever money he could afford. The countryside was very rich in sea-birds and shore-birds, because of the silting up along the coast and also because of the marshes formed by the River Dives. All the local wild-fowlers kept a look-out for rare birds to take to the great house, where the Baron was making a collection of stuffed specimens. The apothecary had been given the responsibility of preparing these specimens, and he was quite good at it.

But he had no one to help him, and he lacked time. If he could find a pupil careful and intelligent enough; he was willing to pay him as soon as the assistant knew his business.

'Take me on, sir!' said Clopinet. 'I'm certain I can learn fast and do well. Why, if you won't be offended, I'll say I know more about birds than you do! Look at this creature, for instance, that you call a sea-peacock. I didn't know its name; but I've seen it a hundred times in its living, free state, and I know how it looks and how it behaves. You wanted to give it the appearance it has when it's fighting: well, it's not quite like this . . . If the thing could be re-shaped, then I'd show you the bird's natural attitude.'

The apothecary was an intelligent man, which meant that he was quick to see intelligence in others. He was

not annoyed in the slightest by Clopinet's criticism. He
said: 'Well, have a try then! The specimen can be re-
shaped, as you put it. That is, the bird's pose can be
altered by bending the wires that replace the bones and
muscles. Go on, have a try! If you spoil the specimen, it
doesn't matter. A ruff isn't such a rarity, after all.'

Pale and almost trembling with excitement, Clopinet
paused while he thought hard in order to remember
accurately. Then, without further hesitation, he seized
the bird, with great delicacy of touch, but also with
great determination. There and then he gave it an
attitude so exactly true to life, and a bearing so proud,
that the apothecary was quite astonished. Nor had
Clopinet damaged a single feather.

'I confess,' said the apothecary, 'that your new pose
looks more natural than mine. But mine looked more
spirited.'

'I beg your pardon, sir?' said Clopinet.

'I mean that mine looked more dangerous. And these
birds are savage creatures!'

'And that's where you're wrong, sir,' Clopinet
answered earnestly. 'Birds are not vicious when hunger
does not force them to do battle. And these birds do not
fight in order to injure each other – and they very rarely
do. No, it's a game they take great pride in playing
before spectators. I'll tell you how they play it. All the
males go off to one side, and all the females to the other,
with their little ones. The males pick on sand-heaps
where they can arrange themselves in line; the females,
on another sandhill, watch. Then the older males say to
the young ones: "Come on, lads, let's see how you can

fight!" And then two young ones start going at each other hammer and tongs, until they collapse from sheer exhaustion; and then two more come together; and so on. Sometimes two pairs fight at the same time, but always one against one, and never a whole group against another group. They are fighting neither for the females nor for food. When the performance is over, they stroll about or feed together, all good friends.'

'You make it sound very likely!' said the apothecary, laughing. 'If you have watched the birds so closely, then I do believe you know more about them than I. And I confess I prefer this ruff as it now is, re-shaped and re-posed by you. I think you are an excellent observer – a born artist, perhaps.'

This meant little to Clopinet; but his heart jumped for joy when the apothecary said to him: 'Come back tomorrow. Yes, I'll teach you the craft, which is really quite easy. You have a feel for it, I think – a natural gift. In due course, if I can, I'll get the Baron at the great house at Platecôte to take you on to work on his collection. Then you'll really learn the natural history of birds; and one day you'll become the curator of the Baron's collection – or of someone else's. Who knows? – You were perhaps born to be a great expert!'

Clopinet understood only one thing: he was going to see birds quite new to him, and he would also learn the names and homelands of birds with whose shape, plumage and habits he was already familiar.

He flew rather than ran home to his father, and easily got his permission to work in 'the bird business', as his father called it. 'Since that's his fancy!' said Farmer

Doucy, smiling at his wife. 'And the apothecary is a worthy man. And I suspect, wife, that you'll not mind your child working so near, where we can see him often.'

Clopinet's mother would rather that the boy never left home at all, but her husband's lightest word – even said with a smile – was law to her. She made haste to agree with him. Besides, this arrangement was so much better than she had feared. She had often trembled at the thought that Clopinet might go back to that Scotland-country, which she believed to be situated at the world's end.

After a month with the apothecary, Clopinet had learnt how to make up the arsenic preparation which preserved the birds from corruption and moth. With great deftness he could remove the skin of any bird, turning it inside out as he did so, as though it were a glove; and he never soiled or ruffled a single feather. He knew exactly which of the tiny bones he needed to keep, and which he must cut out, and how to replace the general bony framework by a system of wires of different thicknesses. He could pick out from the stocks of glass eyes the ones that were right for this fowl or that. He knew how to stuff a bird with tow and keep its exactly right shape. He could sew up the underside with such skill that his stitching became invisible. He could set the bird upright on its feet, and shut or open its wings according to what was needed; and, in giving the grace or individuality of a natural pose, he was a past-master.

The apothecary really wanted only to sell his

apothecary's medicines and medicaments: he would have preferred to rid his laboratory of this work of bird-stuffing. So he was soon thinking that the time had come to get Clopinet into the great house of Platecôte. After all, the boy was really working for the Baron already, although neither the Baron nor the Curé, his close rival in ornithology, knew of Clopinet's existence yet.

The apothecary was a kindly man, as well as a shrewd one. He had Clopinet's interests at heart, as well as his own. He took him off to the great house and personally introduced him to the Baron as a quiet, hardworking boy of real ability and understanding.

'I don't doubt it,' the Baron replied courteously, 'but he's a child. He's clean and minds his manners; but he's a little farm boy who knows nothing.'

'Monsieur le Baron knows all that needs to be

known,' the apothecary said gracefully. 'He will be able to teach the lad what is required. Monsieur le Baron has no child, and could spare some attention to this one, who will become his loyal and devoted servant. I strongly advise Monsieur le Baron not to let this boy slip through his fingers, for Monsieur le Curé will try to get hold of him, once he has seen the work he can do.'

With that, the apothecary opened the box he had brought with him, and set out on the table three different bird-specimens. To each Clopinet had managed to give an appearance so lifelike that the Baron – who knew the different birds well – exclaimed aloud in astonishment and admiration. He said: 'I can certainly see that *you* have not done this really excellent work, Master Apothecary. Can you swear to me that it was really done by this child here?'

'I swear it, Monsieur le Baron.'

'By him, and by him alone?'

'By him alone.'

'Very well, I'll take him on. Leave him here with me. He will never regret having entered my service.'

12

AT THE GREAT HOUSE

On that very day Clopinet was installed at Platecôte. His room, high among the attics of the great house, was tiny, but neat and nice. Even before looking round it, however, he stuck his head out of the window to look at the neighbouring countryside.

The views were splendid, for the house had been built on a hill. Thence could be seen, on one side, the courses of the River Dives and the River Orne, with their woods and gently rolling meadowlands; and, on the other side, the sea and coasts to a great distance. Clopinet recognized at once the jagged peaks of the great cliff; and he saw them even more distinctly, when he used the big Platecôte telescope. This was set up in a viewing turret perched even higher than his own little room. Through this telescope he was overjoyed to make out the Black Cows, which were showing their backs just above the waves. He saw all the inlets, all the hamlets and villages along the coast. He recognized Trouville, and picked out the headland beyond which Honfleur lay hidden. Inland, he could see his own home in the distance – the thatched roof peeped out from among the yellowing leaves of the apple trees.

He felt almost drunk with joy to be thus living right

up in the sky, as it seemed, and to be able to add to his own sharp eyesight the marvellous power of the telescope, a power of vision surely like a bird's!

Next day came another delight: a special room was given over to him as a laboratory and workroom. Here he found already laid out the flasks, various materials, and instruments that the apothecary had assembled and sent for his use. The workroom opened directly into the Baron's museum, and there Clopinet saw, in tall, glass-fronted cupboards, a great number of bird-specimens, both of that region and from abroad. Some were less valuable than others, but all extremely interesting to anyone wanting to master names and classifications.

The Baron now made his appearance, to explain to Clopinet what work he wanted him to do. But Clopinet, plainspoken from a guileless heart, first told him: 'Monsieur le Baron, your collection of birds is not well arranged. Look! Here's a little bird that has been put with these others just because it's little; but that won't do at all! The little bird ought to be next to those big birds over there, because it belongs to the same family – I'm certain of it! The little bird has their same beak, their feet, and it gets its food in the same way: I know it – I recognize it. Or if it's not exactly the same, it has a close family likeness: it must be a cousin or a nephew.'

The Baron encouraged Clopinet to talk on. The boy was not ordinarily a chatterbox at all, but on the subject of birds he always had a great deal to say. The Baron marvelled at the accuracy of his observation and the soundness of his reasoning. The boy had a remarkable memory, too, for in the course of the morning he took

in all the bird-names that the Baron cared to tell him; and he went through them again afterwards without a mistake.

But all at once Clopinet became aware that the Baron was yawning and taking a great many pinches of snuff. Obviously he had wearied of teaching such a little ignoramus.

So thought Clopinet; and he said: 'Monsieur le Baron, it's still too soon for me to enter your service. You would have to teach me everything, and you wouldn't like that. No, I must be able to teach myself, and for that I must learn to read. Let me go to Monsieur le Curé: it's part of his job to be patient with people. When I've learnt to read from him, I'll come back to you.'

'Certainly not!' said the Baron. 'On no account are

you going off to that parish priest! My valet has had
enough education to be able to teach you.'

The valet could read fluently and wrote a good hand.
He knew enough of his native French to write a fair
letter at the dictation of the Baron. The latter was a
scholar and a wit, but of far too good a family to know
how to spell.

Monsieur de La Fleur – that was the valet's name –
had to act the schoolmaster to the little farmer's boy, and
he did it with a bad grace and not very much patience.
With most children, patience is necessary; but for
children, like Clopinet, who are eager to learn and fear
only to see their chance slipping away from them – for
such children even an irritable, lazy teacher will do.
Clopinet himself had a great wish to learn, and he tried
his best not to tire the valet's rather small wish to teach.
By the end of the year Clopinet could read, write and
reckon up as well as his teacher.

This was not enough for Clopinet. The scientific
names of birds were in Latin, and many of the books of
natural history were written in Latin. So he must learn
this language; and he began going privately to the
parish priest. Every Sunday – Clopinet's free day – he
worked on the Curé's collection of stuffed birds, and in
exchange the priest taught him. By the end of another
year, Clopinet had learnt all the Latin he needed.

While he was improving his mind in this way, Clopinet was busy stuffing all the feathered creatures which
came to him at Platecôte. Some were from the neighbouring countryside, some from great distances abroad,
sent or brought by the suppliers and agents of the

Baron. He repaired or renewed those specimens in the Baron's collection which had been ill-done in the first place, or had deteriorated since. He also re-arranged the whole collection more satisfactorily, after discussion – sometimes quite heated – with his patron. The Baron thought himself very knowledgeable, and could not easily admit to being in the wrong. But Clopinet's opinions had been reached by the scrupulous workings of his natural intelligence, and were now maintained with an unshakeable firmness that was part of his character. He always managed to persuade the Baron to his own way of thinking. The Baron, who was no fool, would shrug his shoulders and pretend to be sick of the whole argument and to be giving way for the sake of peace. He would say: 'Oh, do what you like! Over such a trifle I don't propose to vex myself, or to vex you.'

But such things were not really trifles. The parish priest was less rich in specimens than the Baron, but nevertheless he was better informed and more intelligent. And he held Clopinet and his views in the highest esteem. He predicted that – given his chance – the boy had a great future.

Clopinet himself had no vanity and no worldly ambition; no interest in money or in fame. Nothing tempted him, except the things of Nature. He dreamed only of distant travel, discoveries and observations made by himself and himself alone.

Besides, he was always thinking of his hermit's cell on the great cliff. The more he knew of the comfortable life at Platecôte, the more he missed his rocky bed, his wild flowers, the singing of the free birds, and – above all –

their trusting friendship. Sometimes the remembrance of that strange intimacy made his heart contract with longing. He would ask himself: 'Where now are those little sharers of my solitude? Where are my godwits, that imitated so well the bleating of goats and the barking of dogs? Where is the great lonely bittern, that bellowed like a bull? Where are the pretty lapwings with their practical jokes? They borrowed the tailor's voice to scream into my ears *Eighteen! 'Teen! 'Teen!* Where are the curlews, whose soft, children's voices called me in the dark night and made magic wings to grow, my wings of courage?'

Evidently Clopinet no longer believed in spirits of the night. But he looked wistfully back to the time when he thought he could distinguish the very words of his little friends of the black skies and the stormy winds; and he was no happier for his disbelief. The surroundings in which he now found himself certainly did not allow of the supernatural. At that time, many people prided themselves on being very rationalist, even the parish priest. Everything could be explained by reason, or perhaps even explained away altogether. The valet, Monsieur de la Fleur, was particularly scornful of country superstitions.

When Clopinet had reached the age of fifteen to sixteen in the Baron's service, he found that – as far as ornithology went – he had received all the teaching possible in the great house and its neighbourhood. Now he was seized with an irresistible longing to go back to Nature herself to inquire her secrets – those secrets not always to be found in books. His longing unsatisfied, he began to droop and pine, and people remarked how pale he was. He knew what was wrong with him. It was time to consider how he could regain his precious freedom.

He felt grateful to his patron, the Baron, and very much attached to him. Yet he declared to him at last that he must leave him – and leave him for far distant places. Clopinet added the promise, however, that he would collect and bring back with him anything that might be of interest for the Platecôte museum.

The Baron reproached him gently. Did he really propose to leave his service in this way, after all the instruction which – he said – he had given Clopinet? Could he really be so unmindful of all that had been done for him?

In order to keep Clopinet with him, the Baron offered to raise his wages to the same level as de La Fleur's; and he would not expect him to eat in the servants' hall in the future. But Clopinet thought he was well enough paid, and he felt no disgrace in eating with servants. He thanked the Baron, and refused his offers.

'Perhaps,' said the Baron, 'you don't like wearing my livery? Well, I'll pay for a little black suit to be made for you, such as the apothecary wears.'

Clopinet still refused: he thought himself only too richly dressed.

Now the Baron grew angry. He called Clopinet ungrateful and mad. He threatened to wash his hands of him altogether, and declared that he would strike out of his will the little pension that he had intended to leave him.

All was to no avail. Clopinet kissed his hands and
assured him that, disinherited or not, he would always
be devoted and loyal to him. But he would die if he
stayed cooped up as he had been for the last three years.
He was bird-like in needing space and liberty, even at
the price of all miseries imaginable.

The Baron knew when he was beaten; and he
resigned himself. He now dismissed Clopinet with
kindness, paying his full wages and adding to them a
little present of more money. Clopinet would not take
the gift; but, instead, he asked the Baron to let him have
a portable telescope and several instruments. The Baron
gave him these, and insisted upon his keeping the
money, too.

When he saw the Baron so kind and generous,
Clopinet began to think he really was ungrateful. He
threw himself at his benefactor's feet and declared that
he would give up all his dreams of travel. He asked for
leave only for a week, and then, he promised faithfully,
he would come back. Once back, he would try his
hardest to adapt to life in the great house, which, after
all, his patron had made so comfortable for him. The
Baron was deeply moved. He embraced the boy; and
he provided him with all he needed for a week's
expedition.

The day before he left, Clopinet devoted to visiting
his family. Then, on a fine morning in spring, he set out
alone for the great cliff.

Previously he had been so busy working for the
Baron and so bent upon learning from the parish priest,
that he had never allowed himself to waste even an hour

in walking for pleasure. So he had not seen the Black Cows again, and he feared to find what ravages the sea might have made in his absence. At the great house and at the parish priest's, he had heard talk of massive landslides; but from the look-out turret at Platecôte he had seen that the jagged peaks of the cliff were still visible. He decided not to believe half of what he had heard.

For his expedition he wore a countryman's thick smock, stout shoes, and gaiters of stiff canvas; and on his head he wore a woollen cap against the worst of the winds. On his back he carried a strong, capacious travelling bag, which held his instruments, one or two reference books on birds, his telescope and some food.

He reached the dunes quickly, but not by following the shore. This was blocked in various places by land-

slides of marl. As he went forward, keeping roughly to the middle of the slopes, he saw a very marked change in those fissured masses. Where plants had grown before, there was nothing now but mud – very difficult to cross without sinking right in. Where there had been softness, there was now firm ground covered with vegetation.

Clopinet could no longer easily find his way. The familiar paths, which he had made and which he alone knew, had disappeared. All over again he had to learn which routes to take, and work out new ways of avoiding the deep cracks and precipices.

At last he reached the great cliff. It still stood, indeed; but its sides were now cut sheer. They forbade him to climb to his cave-house.

13

A NIGHT OF STORM

He simply had to give up.

He had felt such joy at the prospect of repossessing his eyrie; and now –

Now he gave up.

Or nearly so. But then, in a kind of frenzy, he began struggling to reach his cave-house, his dear home. He tried now this way, now that – any new way that might lead him upwards. At last he succeeded in finding an ascent that seemed perhaps not too difficult, not too perilous. He risked himself on it . . .

And at last he reached familiar rocky terrain. He came to his garden again, his ravine-walk, his spy-hole, and his cave-house, all more or less intact. He felt a deep content.

At once he busied himself settling in. First he had thoroughly to clean out his old home, for birds had left droppings and other traces. He cut several armfuls of dried sea-rushes and lit a fire to clear the air. He burnt juniper berries to scent it.

Now he was ready to make his bed. This was quickly done with dried grasses, which he cut and then spread in position.

He ate a simple meal, and afterwards took a nap. He

stretched himself out on the turf of his wild garden. He
fell asleep among the flowers he had always loved and
that bloomed around him more beautifully than ever.

He slept soundly, for he had risen early that morning
and was tired out with trudging across the broken
dunes. He woke, fully rested. At once his mind turned to
the ascent of the topmost heights of the great cliff: he
meant to find out if the same birds still made their
home there. With a great deal more struggling and a
great deal more risk as well, he managed the climb.
Arrived at the heights, however, he saw no sign of nests,
and there was not a single feather to be found. The
hernshaws had deserted the site — surely a sign that it
was in danger of collapse: their instinct warned them of
it.

Where had the birds taken refuge, then? Clopinet's
interest was not for the money he could make in selling
feathers, since he felt himself rich enough already. But
he would have liked to see his old friends again. He
wondered if they would recognize him after such a long
absence. It seemed hardly likely.

Looking all about him, he saw that a great crack had
opened on the downward slope of the cliff. Cautiously
he edged his way into it, and soon found it to be like a
street that had been newly carved out in his deserted
city. The way led him downwards until it became partly
choked with huge boulders; and now he realized with
astonishment that he must be quite near his cave-house.

And the rocks now round about him were white
with bird-droppings.

He needed no further encouragement to search for

nests. He found a great number, in which the eggs, now warmed by the sun, would at nightfall be brooded by the birds themselves. Round about were many feathers of the kind he knew so well.

So the night herons had moved house! Their choosing to settle so close to his own domain reassured Clopinet: if their instinct were right, his home in the cranny of the cliff was still safe. Altogether, Clopinet was well pleased with his discoveries. He easily made his way back from the nesting-site to his cave-house by climbing the ridge that separated them. Home again, he thought with satisfaction of his old friends so close at hand.

Clopinet was a true lover of solitude. This one day in his wilderness seemed to him a reward for a long exile bravely endured. Now he was at home again on the dunes: he could roam their whole extent, and learn by heart their new geography. Now he greeted again his dear Black Cows, covered as always with their shellfish. Now he tasted again the delights of bathing in the sea; and now again he watched all the birds – those that lived on the shore and those that stayed only a short time, on their way elsewhere.

He could hardly learn more about these familiar birds. There was only one thing he could not decide: whether these were not the same individual birds that he had known, or whether they simply had no remembrance of him. They seemed not to recognize him at all, and would not approach when he offered bread. All the same, bread was still a great treat, and, as soon as he had gone even a little way off, they pounced on the crumbs he had scattered, and quarrelled over them with loud cries.

Clopinet still hoped to gentle the birds and make them as tame as before. His leave was short, but he would spend the whole of it here on the cliff. It was the place he most wanted to be, although he could hardly have explained his passion.

Yet Clopinet was not the same boy that had lived in the wilds for six months, those years ago. Now he was more or less educated; and he knew the why and wherefore of many things that before had simply given him pleasure. He had loved the sea, the rocks, the birds, the flowers and the clouds in the sky, before he had ever known that such things were supposed to be 'beautiful'. Now he was glad to think that he had loved the things of Nature before ever attempting to understand and describe them.

It seemed as if that same Nature were welcoming back her child with a celebration such as he had been treated to three years before. On the first evening of his settling on the cliff, he saw the sun set amid a great heaping up of black clouds edged with red fire; and the sea was one phosphorescence . . .

At last, turning from this spectacle, Clopinet went back into his cave-house for the night. Soon the wind began to rise, and the celebration outside became noisy and rough. Torrents of rain streamed down round the little hermitage; but the moon, shining steadily on the drops of water, studded with green diamonds the foliage which festooned the entrance.

In the midst of the din of this storm, Clopinet slept

happily. He even enjoyed the excitement of being woken from time to time by crashes of thunder. One thunder clap was so violent, however, that he felt the shock of it through all his body, and – without knowing how it happened – he found himself out of bed and on his feet. A myriad plaintive cries filled the air above him, and in an instant he felt himself flailed by a great number of wings that wildly but soundlessly beat around him in his cave-house. The colony of his bird-neighbours had been struck by lightning. The females, distraught and terrified, had left their shattered eggs, and, borne along by the winds of the storm, they came sweeping down into Clopinet's garden and right into his very cave-house, with a clamour of wailing and lamenting.

Clopinet felt the utmost pity for the poor creatures, and was careful not to drive them from him. Instead, he managed to get back into bed and even to sleep with the birds all around him, some stretched, more dead than alive, across his very bed.

As soon as day broke, all those that could flew away; but many could not. They were broken-winged, or partly blinded, or even dead or dying. To the best of his ability, Clopinet tended his unhappy visitors; and then he went to see the extent of the damage done to the colony on the nesting-site. He saw the mother birds seeking their eggs in vain, and heard their outcry and lamenting. He tried to repair some of the nests; but the electrical discharge from the storm had cooked what it had not broken.

The surviving birds saw that there was no longer

hope for them in that place. They began calling to each other with strange cries of distress, and gradually assembled on one of the great rocks. There they appeared to take counsel together briefly. Then, with what sounded like sobs of farewell, they took flight over the sea and disappeared into the mists. It was impossible to see what became of them.

Clopinet watched for their return the next day, and the days following; but in vain. He decided that they had said good-bye perhaps forever to that inhospitable coast. So he turned all his attention to his sick birds. In a short while, they had become tame. They ate from his hand and let themselves be touched, scratched and warmed by him. They began walking round him and settling down, some in his cave-house to sleep, others in his garden, to be revived by the sunshine there. Strangely, they seemed to have forgotten the disaster that had befallen their offspring: they made no attempt to see what had become of them. They answered by sad, harsh little calls the loud summons of the others who were leaving. They resigned themselves to domestic life as to a new kind of existence against which it was useless to protest.

Now Clopinet was able to study something which had always fascinated him: the degree of intelligence which develops in animals when instinct alone is not enough for self-preservation. He spent a large part of the day watching the convalescent birds, all more or less maimed, who had resigned themselves to his care. The rest of the day he went to and fro about the cliff, gathering up bird-visitors of other species. He found

them lying everywhere. The storm had brought some that he had not until now seen from close to: spoonbills, cormorants and little bitterns. By the evening, they filled his cave-house; and he had to give them the remains of his bread and go to bed supperless.

The next morning he hurried off to find himself something to eat at Auberville, the village where he had shopped for food in the past. He also brought back with him provisions for his sick-bay.

During that day there were some deaths and some recoveries. He went out again to gather up any wounded birds on the heights. While he was there, he could see that some birds, now restored to health and freedom, were watching him as he went about, in order to pick up the crumbs of bread he dropped. A few days were enough to make them as unafraid as in the past. Clopinet thought that he recognized, in those that most quickly became tame, the same birds that had once already been gentled by him.

He noticed that such birds, who became quite used to coming near him, could still remain independent-spirited. In this they were very different from those who had suffered wounds or loss of consciousness as a result of the storm of lighting. These quickly came to depend on Clopinet; and they grew all-trusting to the point of pestering him with their attentions. They no longer enjoyed the freedom of flight or, indeed, of any swift movement, and they seemed to have developed instead a kind of selfishness and insatiable greed. Clopinet preferred the other birds, who remained fully active and held themselves proudly. He gave more care to those birds that had more need of him, but he could not help rather despising the too easy surrender of their bird-natures.

Nevertheless, pity made Clopinet tend them closely: he hoped eventually to fit them all for wild life again. He was so well practised in the reconstruction of the bony framework of birds that he knew their anatomy well; and he succeeded with marvellous skill in mending broken legs and wings. The birds thus put to rights again were able, after only a few days, to seek their own food. But they were badly received by those already at liberty, and came back to Clopinet quite abashed, to take refuge at his feet. Then Clopinet had to ward them off, and at the same time roundly to scold the others, as arrogant and ill-mannered creatures, for wanting to peck out their comrades' feathers or tear them wholly to pieces. He had to take part in some strange skirmishes; and you can imagine with what interest he observed all the airs and attitudes of these feathered personages.

By the end of the week Clopinet was thinking of leaving the cliff and going back to his patron. In any case, it was high time to think of beating a retreat, for the cliff had been much damaged in the last storm. Close to a hernshaw's nest that had been struck by lightning, a new fissure had opened; and the marl, almost liquefied by the rains, was beginning to ooze down towards Clopinet's garden.

The threat to his garden grieved Clopinet. The little hollow was full of good earth, chiefly humus. Here he had taken pleasure in growing the prettiest plants from the near neighbourhood – broom, handsome viper's bugloss, yellowwort with its sunny flowers, sea-lavender of pure lilac tint and graceful shape, and pretty sea-bindweeds with their pink corollas striped with white and their thick, glossy leaves. The bindweeds spread flowers and foliage to the very edge of sands wet daily by the tide.

While Clopinet had been away, his flower-garden had flourished and spread itself to the threshold of his cave-house. Now all of it was going to disappear forever! The unrelenting, invading marl would take it over; and the marl was heavy, compacted, sterile in itself and steriliz-ing, when not skilfully mixed – as farmers mix it – with earths of a different kind. After some time, or perhaps quite quickly, under the action of external forces such as rain and storm, the great mass must overwhelm both garden and cave-house, and bury them.

Clopinet was too alert and too well used to observing the slightest movement of the marl to be afraid of being taken by surprise. All the same, he slept nowadays with – so to speak – an eye open and an ear cocked; and he judged the days carefully. He would say: 'This is another fine day, and that will help to dry the mud. But, if it rains tomorrow, I may have to move out quickly and see the end of this little world of mine.'

In expectation of this, and to save his birds from further disaster, he resolved to take them back with him to the parish priest at Dives. The Curé liked to keep living creatures about him, while the Baron of Platecôte preferred them dead and stuffed. The priest was more of a naturalist; the Baron more of a collector. Clopinet felt certain that the priest would take good care of his birds.

He went off inland to cut suitable sticks, and with these he set about weaving a basket big enough to carry all his friends without danger of suffocation. He thought the laden basket would be too heavy for him to carry by himself, as some of the birds were very large. So he went off again and hired a donkey. He drove the beast up as near as possible to the entrance of his garden. Now he was ready to set off the next morning.

14

THE CASTAWAY

The night was stormy, and the marl gained a great deal of ground.

Clopinet had to rise before dawn. He fed his invalid birds, and then he fed the donkey which was to carry them. He gathered the birds together and put them carefully into his basket, now lined with grass. Then he loaded the basket on to the packsaddle of the donkey.

They were quite ready. Helping the donkey where he could, Clopinet led it down the cliff and right to the sea's edge.

He had timed their departure exactly: the tide was just beginning to ebb, and would allow them to go by the shore in the direction of Dives. But he had not reckoned with the donkey. The animal was seized with terror when it heard the sound of the sea so close – it was still too dark for anything to be visible. It stopped dead; its whole body trembled; it put its ears back, and it refused to budge. Clopinet was very patient. He did not beat the donkey, but instead petted it and coaxed it: he was giving it time to get used to the sound of the waves.

Meanwhile, Clopinet was looking towards the great Black Cow, which still lifted its back above the waters; and he thought he saw something extraordinary on that back. There was not enough light yet for him to make out what the thing was. It had what looked like a small body with long legs that moved. Clopinet thought it must be a gigantic octopus; and curiosity made him peer very intently. The thing was moving about all the time, now one leg, now another; but the main part of the body seemed glued to the rock. All the same, Clopinet feared the mysterious creature might detach itself before he could observe it properly and decide exactly what it was. Quickly he took off his clothes and threw them on to the donkey's back. Then he went into the sea; but the swell was so heavy that he could advance only by hanging on first to one and then another of the underwater rocks. Fortunately he knew the rocks and their position like the back of his hand.

At last he came close enough to see that this was no octopus but a man, who clung tightly to the top of the Great Cow, with unmistakable signs of distress. But what an odd-looking man! He was so weird in appearance that, even in his astonishment, Clopinet's mind flew to that monstrosity of a tailor who had been the terror of his early childhood. He alone could be as hideous as this creature with the huge head and the long bony limbs plainly visible through the sodden clothes that clung to them. As Clopinet made his way towards him, he thought he heard a voice that cried: 'Help! Help!'

Clopinet reached the last rock before the Great Cow itself. Only a very short distance now separated him from the castaway. He could see clearly, by the swiftly growing daylight, that this was indeed the abominable tailor whose hateful memory had haunted him for the three years since they last met.

He shouted: 'Don't move! Wait there for me!'

Too late! Either Left-hand-thread did not hear him or the ebbing tide carried him away in spite of himself. With a supreme effort he made as if to stretch out his long arms towards Clopinet – and let go his hold! In a twinkling he was swept away by the waves that swirled around the great rock, and disappeared beneath the waters.

Clopinet was still on his own rock, where he had paused to take breath. There he remained for an instant, irresolute in mind and as if frozen by the fear of death. People think fast at such times: at once Clopinet realized that, if he went to the tailor's help, the terrified wretch would clutch at him and cling to him like an octopus indeed, prevent his swimming and drag him down with him below the water. To die thus so suddenly – to die in such a ghastly manner – to die when he was still so young and eager for life and all its mysteries – to die trying uselessly to save the life of a creature as sly, as spiteful, as altogether vile as that tailor – oh! it was sheer madness!

So Clopinet hesitated for an instant – but only for the shortest of all instants. For at once there seemed to sound melodiously in his ear the voices that he knew so well: the voices of his little friends, the winged spirits of the sea. Clear yet gentle, almost caressing, the voices spoke: 'Your wings! Open your wings! We are with you!'

Clopinet felt great wings of courage open and spread

wide like the wings of a sea-eagle, and he leapt into the boiling sea. He never knew how he reached the tailor and seized hold of him in the midst of blinding spray. He fought with him and overcame him, and then, with superhuman effort, overcame the huge wave that was carrying them out to sea. Finally, he got them both back to the Great Cow, where he dropped down exhausted on top of the body of his castaway, by now unconscious.

It had all happened as if in a dream; and Clopinet's superior education nowadays told him that it could not possibly have happened at all in reality. Yet he was utterly sure that his good spirits had helped him, as of old. He raised himself up from the rock to call aloud: 'Thank you – oh, thank you, dear, dear friends!'

He turned his attention to the tailor. He rolled him over on to his stomach and held him in that position, head downwards, to make him bring up the water he had swallowed. He rubbed him vigorously, until he saw that he was breathing again. After five minutes, Left-hand-thread revived, and tried to speak; but he could give only loud, gasping cries while he struggled against a last choking-fit. He was beside himself. He wanted to jump back into the sea in order to reach dry land faster. He behaved like a madman. Clopinet succeeded in keeping him where he was only by hitting him hard with the flat of his hand; and that finally brought him to his senses.

'Trust me!' Clopinet said to him, when he could make the tailor understand anything. 'In a few moments this rock will be high and dry, and we shall get back to shore just by walking there. I've managed to warm you a little, haven't I? If you get cold again, you'll die.'

Left-hand-thread gave in to this reasoning. And, just as Clopinet had said, within a quarter of an hour, they were staggering ashore.

The resourceful Clopinet at once began gathering dried grasses, and with these kindled a fire on a ridge of the dune which the tide never reached. In front of this blaze, Left-hand-thread began to dry out, and at the same time munched the bread that Clopinet gave him.

Only then could the tailor explain to Clopinet how, in spite of his horror of the sea, he had let himself be trapped and swept away. He told Clopinet: 'There's something I must confess to you. I live poorly by my trade, and I was filled with envy when I saw you decked out in three of those precious hernshaw feathers. From that day, my one aim was to find the hiding-place of your birds. I saw so many flying over and around that accursed cliff; but I dared not risk climbing it. I walk and climb very nicely, thank you; but God has not made me over-brave. I dared not try on my own; and I dared not, like you, make a pact with the Devil.'

'Master Tailor,' said Clopinet, passing him his flask, 'drink up, and get your ideas straight. You're an idiot to believe in the Devil; and when you claim that I've sold myself to him, I tell you – without offending you at all, I trust – that you're a stupid liar.'

The tailor was by nature quarrelsome and ready for any fray, but now he hung his head and mumbled excuses. He knew who had the upper hand.

He began again: 'My dear Master Clopinet, I owe it to you that I am still the ornament of this world. I am

grateful to you; and as for the ladies – they will bless you.'

'Since you are so witty about yourself, and good-tempered enough not to mind being laughed at, I forgive you,' said Clopinet.

But, in fact, the tailor was not joking. He really thought himself a fine figure of a man, and was sure that the ladies all found him attractive and fought for his attention. He said as much to Clopinet.

At this, Clopinet was seized with such a fit of laughing that he actually fell over and lay on his back, gasping and guffawing, holding his sides and drumming his feet. The tailor would have got into one of his rages if he had dared, but he dared not. He went on with his story.

'It was one of these affairs of the heart that proved my undoing,' said he. 'Oh, you can laugh; but it's only too true that I left my part of the country in obedience to the wish of a certain widow. Her wish was to marry me. She was not in her first youth; but she led me to believe that she was rich. I was on the very point of agreeing to her proposal. Then I discovered that she hadn't a sou, not even enough to pay a miserable little debt I'd happened to run up at the tavern. So I ditched her and left her. I was coming back this way with a heavy heart, a light pocket and an empty stomach; I even had to beg a crust from the baker at Villers.

'That was yesterday evening; and it was then that the idea came to me of looking for hernshaw feathers – I'd always dreamed of them. The baker told me you'd sold yours for three thousand silver crowns to the Baron at Platecôte, and that he had taken you on as his servant and then made you his heir. At least, that was the story going the rounds.

'So then I took it into my head that – whatever the risk to life or limb – I would search out those hernshaws. I knew that they could often be seen flying about here, and that they would have to be caught before daylight, when they leave the sea-shore. So I left Villers at midnight, thinking to reach the Black Cows before the tide did. But I can only suppose that cuckoo of a baker made me late. Perhaps he gave me a drop too much to drink – for he's a man of wit and learning, and he enjoys the company of educated folk like myself. He did not object to my trying his cider, as we chatted the evening away. Well, the cider or the cuckoo or the Devil himself had a hand in it: I was caught unawares by the tide before daybreak and swept on to that rock where, without you, I should have perished.'

'Or rather,' retorted Clopinet, 'where, if only you'd kept your head and used your wits, you could have stayed without danger until the tide had gone down. Anyway, here you are now, safe and sound. Now take these two silver crowns, and be off with you. No offence, but I've had enough of your company.'

The tailor thanked him over and over again. He would have kissed Clopinet's hands, if he had been allowed to.

The tide was far out by now. The donkey's nervousness had vanished, and he was quite ready to carry to Dives the menagerie intended for the parish priest there. Clopinet had also collected a good many plants that his friend the apothecary had asked him to bring back if he could: there was a big bundle of them tied behind the donkey. The tailor had been told to be off, but he could not bear to go. He lingered, eyeing the cage and the bundle of plants most inquisitively – and most covetously.

Clopinet said to him: 'You could make yourself useful and also earn a little something by gathering plants like these. But as for the birds of the dune, of whatever kind, I absolutely forbid you to set traps for them or to disturb them in any way as they sit on their eggs.'

The tailor listened, but then replied with a kind of timid cunning: 'All the same, the birds of the sea-shore belong to everybody. In your cage there, you have the most magnificent hernshaws. You've caught them; they

belong to you; but there must be plenty more where they came from. If you felt any pity for a poor man, you would tell him in what place the birds hide themselves away during the day, and how a poor man might reach such a place without getting killed. For, after all, *you've* just done it, and you've just made a rich haul for yourself.'

'Master Left-hand-thread,' answered Clopinet, 'you still want to do just what I have forbidden you, and you don't mind going against my express wishes, in spite of all I've done for you. But did you not hear a strange sound just now? Listen! Listen to what awaits you if you scale the great cliff . . .'

'What then?' the tailor asked doubtfully.

'Do you hear nothing?'

'I think I can hear thunder beginning from the direction of Honfleur.'

'That's no thunder. That's the sound of the cliff's starting to fall. It's high time to leave – come on!'

Clopinet made his donkey trot, and the terrified tailor hurried ahead even faster, to put a safe distance between himself and danger. Suddenly he halted in abject fear: the rumblings behind him had changed into a tremendous roar. He turned, and was in time to see a whole face of the cliff collapse with enormous boulders being hurled far out into the sea. Within seconds, before his appalled eyes, a herd of white cows had joined the existing herd of black ones.

Clopinet, too, had stopped and turned. He saw tumbling down with the rocks the ruined masonry of his beloved hermitage and observatory. He turned to the tailor and said bitterly: 'Back there I had a country cottage, a garden, and – for neighbours – as many hernshaws as the heart could desire. Go and take possession of it all, if you wish!'

The tailor was stunned and cowed by what had happened. Dumbly he shook his head. He was forever cured of his greedy dreams of scaling cliffs and catching sea-birds. He slunk off, and Clopinet did not see him again.

Clopinet continued on his way with his laden donkey, sad at heart. He had loved his hermitage, as one might love a human being. The hardships he had endured, the dangers he had braved, the dreams – both delightful and fearful – that he had dreamed there: all these now seemed to him to have bound him to the dear place. Now those ties of love were destroyed forever by a disaster that he had long foreseen, dreaded, and been powerless to prevent. He had been a guest of Nature, but Nature had not always been kind; she had rough and ready ways that could be mistaken for cruel whims; her laws had to be understood. 'And always we must love Nature,' Clopinet said to himself, 'for, after all, what she takes away with one hand, she gives with another. And some day I shall find again some hidey-hole, some secret place, where I can live alone with her.'

Clopinet deliberately loitered along the shore. He was enjoying his last day of freedom; and he had decided not to arrive in Dives before evening, so that people should not see his load of birds.

Under cover of dusk he carried all his birds to the presbytery, where they were welcomed with delight by the Curé. Clopinet begged him not to let the Baron know where the splendid gift came from.

'I'll see to that!' cried the priest. 'He shall never know of it. For, if he did, I'm positive he wouldn't rest until he'd snatched from me every one of these lovely, living creatures to mummify them. He shan't see them, rest assured of that.'

Clopinet left the priest and his servant hard at work to make their new guests comfortable. He went on to the apothecary, to whom he delivered the plants. Then, at last, he returned to the great house at Platecôte, where he went to bed with a full heart.

15

GOODBYE TO CLOPINET

The next day the Baron found Clopinet back in his old place in the laboratory-workroom. He looked well, and seemed cured of whatever had been the matter with him.

Two days later the poor boy was as pale and despondent as ever before. The Baron questioned him closely, and at last Clopinet came out with it: 'Monsieur le Baron, you must let me go. I can't live here any longer. I thought that fresh air and exercise for those few days would cure me; but I was wrong. I need more time than that. I need a year, perhaps more – I don't know. Please, Monsieur le Baron, stop being so kind to me: I'm not worthy of it. But don't turn from me altogether – don't hate me, for then unhappiness would prevent my making good use of your gift of freedom.'

When the Baron saw Clopinet's distress, he acted like the good-hearted man he could be: he comforted the boy and promised he would never cease to take the warmest interest in him. For the Baron had given way before the inevitable: he was resigned to seeing Clopinet go away for a long time – perhaps never to return, for a life of travel is full of hazard. But he did insist that Clopinet should freely open his heart to him, for he suspected there was still some concealment. He simply could not understand this love of solitude.

'Very well,' said Clopinet, 'I'll tell you everything, at the risk of seeming either a fool or a madman. I love birds; but – let's be clear about this – I love birds that *live*, and I feel that I must live with them. I like to see birds in paintings, for a painting gives an impression of life. It even seems to me that one day I could represent in line and colour the creatures that I shall have got to know so well.

'But the stuffing of dead birds has become hateful to me. To live among corpses, to dissect that pitiable dead flesh, to do the job of an embalmer – oh, I can bear it no longer! It seems to me that I breathe death, and that I shall end up as a mummy. I know you admire the handsome bearing and glossiness of plumage that I give to the birds I work on. But the ghosts of those birds haunt me in my dreams and plead for life again, which I cannot give them. And when I have to spend an evening among the show-cases, I seem to hear them knocking on the glass of their prisons with their beaks, begging for liberty for their wings – those wings that I have bound with wires of steel and brass. Oh yes, those ghosts fill me with horror, and I am horrified at myself for having created them. At least, I have not to reproach myself with their deaths, for I have only once killed a bird – one bird only – and that was for food, driven as I was by hunger. I have never been able to forgive myself for that death, and I swore never to kill again. All the same, it's true that I live by the deaths of all those birds that I prepare and stuff as specimens. That knowledge torments me, hounds me like a remorse.

'And besides that . . . Besides that . . . There's something else that I dare hardly — that perhaps I simply don't know how to tell you . . .'

'What is there yet to tell?' asked the Baron. 'You must tell me all: I am your good friend.'

'Very well,' said Clopinet. 'Hear me then. On the sea and on the shore there are bird-voices that speak to me, and that none but I can understand. Of course, birds speak to birds, with calls that express love, fear, anger, anxiety. This is different: these are bird-voices that speak to me alone, and I understand what the voices say. In some crisis, when I don't know what it is right to do, my bird-voices advise me. I have come to believe that we are surrounded by good spirits who take on this form or that, in order to help us and guide us; and my good spirits take on bird-forms and bird-voices. I don't claim that such spirits work miracles, but they cause *us* to work miracles. They influence us, and so turn natural human selfishness and cowardice into self-sacrifice and soaring courage. My bird-voices are the voices of Nature, and they have cast a good spell upon me: I can no longer live out of earshot of them. Here they never speak to me; and from here you must let me go. Be sure the voices will send me back to you one day (as once they sent me back to my own family), and then I shall dutifully report to you on my researches and discoveries. But let me follow my bird-voices, for now they seem to call me: they call me to be a scholar — a scholar that learns from Nature herself.'

The Baron thought that Clopinet talked sense up to a

point; but, all the same, he believed him to be a prey to sick fancies. The boy would certainly benefit from the activity and bustle of travel.

The Baron did everything he could to make Clopinet's first sea-crossing as easy as possible. He provided him with all he needed in the way of money, clothes and instruments of various kinds. He saw him aboard one of the big boats that plied two or three times a year between Dives and Honfleur. At Honfleur Clopinet, now on his own, embarked for England. Thence he went into Scotland, Ireland and the other islands round about.

In the wildest and most desolate of places Clopinet felt free and happy as a bird. Nothing escaped his observant eyes; he noted down everything of interest.

Nor did he forget his promise to the Baron. At the end of his year he returned, bringing with him a rich store of first-hand observations. His findings often ran quite contrary to the accepted opinions of the naturalists of the time; but they were not the less accurate and shrewd, for all that.

The following year, after spending a few weeks with his family and friends, Clopinet went on his travels again. This time he went to Switzerland, Germany, and as far as Poland, Russia and Turkey. Later, he visited the north of Russia and parts of Asia. Everywhere he went he bought up birds that the local people had killed when they went wild-fowling; and he prepared specimens and sent them back to the Baron, whose collection soon became one of the finest in France.

But always Clopinet kept to the oath he had sworn to kill nothing and to have nothing killed for his use. This was an obsession with him, and by it, no doubt, science may have lost some valuable specimens which – if he had been less scrupulous – he could have obtained. On the other hand, he enriched scientific knowledge with much detailed and quite new information, correcting mistaken ideas until then accepted without question. The Baron had no cause for complaint. For a long time he took to himself the honour of all the discoveries made by his pupil, and he published his notes as works of scientific research – in which he quite forgot to mention Clopinet's name. Clopinet did not mind, however, for he had no personal ambition and was perfectly happy as long as he could satisfy his passion for the study of Nature.

The Baron achieved a certain reputation, which had
been the main object of his outlay of money and all his
schemes. But, at least, he was not ungrateful to Clopinet.
When the Baron died, he left everything to him by his
will. The Baron's nephews thereupon started legal
proceedings against this jumped-up little know-all, who
– according to them – had wormed his way into the
confidence of the dead man. The will had been properly
made, and Clopinet would probably have won his case.
But he hated disputes, and so he settled out of court,
accepting the first compromise arrangement that was
offered him. This left him with the great house itself and
its museum and enough land to live off in a modest way;
and he could afford to travel, too, provided he did not
expect luxury – which he had never wanted, anyway.

Clopinet thought himself lucky in every way. He

could travel all over the world, while his family and Uncle Laquille's family lived in the great house. Here he returned from time to time to see to the collection of his benefactor, the Baron – he looked on this as a sacred trust.

Clopinet began to grow old in the ceaseless to-and-fro of his travelling. For whole years together he would disappear and his relatives would receive no news of him: he was staying in places so cut-off and wild that it was impossible for him to communicate with the outside world. Then he would reappear, quiet and serene, sweet-natured, helpful to others, and generous even beyond his means. Other naturalists who met him on his distant expeditions told stories of his goodness of heart and of his quite extraordinary courage. He himself never spoke of his exploits.

For a long time he lived without any failing in health and strength; but then over-tiredness and the intense cold which he had had to endure in studying the habits of the eider-duck in Lapland made him lame in one leg, as he had been in early childhood. He could no longer indulge in a great deal of exercise, as in the past. He began to think that he probably had not many more years to live, and so he busied himself in sending off to various museums all the bird-specimens in the collection at the great house. He also sent to the museums a mass of notes and observations, all without his name attached, which the experts valued very highly, even without knowing from whom they came.

Most naturalists want to appear before the public in some way and get a name for themselves: Clopinet liked to hide himself away. But he could not hide himself from the country-people: they knew him and loved him and respected him. They called him Monsieur le Baron Clopinet, and would have jumped into the sea to please him.

So he lived beloved and happy; and, in his last days, he spent his spare time in making exquisite bird-drawings which, after his death, were much prized and fetched the highest prices.

When failing strength and a certain presentiment warned him that he was nearing his end, he longed once more to see his great cliff. He was still not very old, and his family felt no great anxiety on his account. His old friends, the apothecary and the parish priest, were older than he, but still hale and hearty; and they offered to go with him to the great cliff. He thanked them, but asked to be allowed to go alone. He promised not to go far along the shore. His liking for solitude was well known, and nobody wanted to hinder his pleasure.

When evening came, he did not return. His brothers, his nephews and his friends began to be anxious for him. They set off with torches; the priest and the apothecary bringing up the rear of the search-party. All that night they searched. All the next day they combed the coast; and they made inquiries all the days that followed. But the dunes kept their secrets; the sea cast up no corpse.

Then, one day, an old woman went shrimping along the shore at dawn. Afterwards, she declared she had seen a great sea-bird, the like of which she had never known before. The strange bird skimmed just over her head, and, as it did so, it cried with the voice of Monsieur le Baron Clopinet: 'Farewell, good people! Never grieve on my account, for I have found my wings again.'

AFTERWORD

GEORGE SAND AND HER BIRDS

George Sand (1804–76) was not only one of the best-known French writers of her time, but also a most spectacular – even notorious – woman. That does not concern us here. In her childhood and in old age she lived, not in Paris, but on her family estate of Nohant, in the valley of the River Indre. In old age she still enjoyed literary society and wrote abundantly, but she also devoted herself to her two little granddaughters, Aurore and Gabrielle, and to her garden and the countryside and the countrypeople, who loved her.

In the early summer of 1872 the two little girls had been suffering from whooping-cough. George Sand made up a family party of the children, their parents and their grandmother (herself) to visit the Normandy coast for the sea-air and the bathing. The party stayed first at Trouville and then at Cabourg; and they were delighted with their holiday. All coughs vanished.

The fifteen miles or so along the coast between the two places of stay provide the whole background of the story of Clopinet, told to please the two little girls. Here, among those strangely formed sea-banks that seem to be now cliffs crumbling into dunes, now dunes steep and crannied like cliffs – here Clopinet is imagined as living his Crusoe-like existence.

In December 1872 *La Revue des Deux Mondes* published *Les Ailes de Courage*, described as a tale of fantasy and also (in the Contents) as 'the story of a naturalist'. The story is dedicated to Aurore and Gabrielle.

The hero, Clopinet, has a great deal in common – significantly, I think – with a friend of George Sand and her family: Gustave Tourangin, an amateur naturalist. In a letter of 1868 (published in *Nouvelles Lettres d'un Voyageur*) George Sand sketches his character and gifts. He was nicknamed *Micro* because he was always peering at natural specimens through a microscope. He was keenly interested in birds, and he reminded George Sand of a bird. He was like a shore-bird, she said: slow-seeming and apparently lazy; in reality, tireless. He had a gaze with 'je ne sais quoi d'*ailé*' – a *winged* look. She tried to launch him on some kind of ornithological career, by securing for him a job at the Museum of Natural History in Paris. Here he stuffed bird-specimens, just like Clopinet at Platecôte; and George Sand said his were the most lifelike she had seen. But after only a few months he sickened of the work – again, like Clopinet – and left Paris to return to his family in the country. Like Clopinet, he always allowed his collections, observations and discoveries to be used by anyone interested. He had no worldly ambition; and his life henceforth slipped by in what George Sand calls 'une sorte de contemplation attentive'.

Gustave Tourangin, still only in his fifties, died early in 1872 – only a few months before the Normandy holiday and the writing of the story of Clopinet. He must have been in George Sand's mind that summer, remembered with sadness, affection, admiration and perhaps – if she had been honest with herself – with a recollection of exasperation. For Gustave Tourangin had never achieved what, in George Sand's opinion, he should have done – what she had tried to manoeuvre him into achieving. Clopinet had the gifts of Gustave, but he also developed the *courage* which the actual man clearly lacked: the courage to strike out from his family and use his gifts to make an independent career for himself.

George Sand herself was not really a naturalist – although she much enjoyed botanizing. The birds that throng the pages of *Les Ailes de Courage* are observed with vivid interest, but not always with accuracy. Perhaps some were not observed in Normandy itself; perhaps, indeed, some were not really observed at first-hand at all. Her birds are not always easy to identify by description. In chapter 7 of my version, the 'very large birds' that seemed to have 'the habit of sleeping far out at sea' may well be great northern divers. What about the next kind to be described, the nocturnal birds that came 'wheeling about on the air-currents' down from the heights of the dune? Could George Sand have been thinking – but not at all exactly – of the short-eared owl?

Her naming of birds must sometimes have been from local usage. Her *alouettes de mer* (sea-larks), which are waders of some kind, may be dunlin. (In England, a Sussex name for a dunlin is *sand-lark*.) Her *hirondelles de mer* (sea-swallows) are almost certainly terns, although she describes a way of feeding the young which is not normal. Her *perdrix de mer* (sea-partridge) must be the pratincole (*Glareola pratincola*).

The greatest puzzle is set by some of the most important birds in the story: the night herons (*Nycti-corax nycticorax*). Their French name is *héron bihoreau*, or just *bihoreau*; but George Sand's Normandy peasants also use the name *roupeau*. These two names were really alternatives until the nineteenth century, when *roupeau* began to be old-fashioned and little used. I decided to employ the old English word *hernshaw* (which simply means a heron) for *roupeau*.

George Sand describes the night herons and their behaviour as though she had observed them closely and often – as though Clopinet had so observed them, a hundred years before; and yet it is very unlikely that anyone, in either period, could have seen them nesting on that Normandy coast. They are birds of wetlands and woods, not of the sea and the sea-shore; and they only rarely come so far north in France. But perhaps George Sand knew them from her valley of the Indre. A century ago there were more undrained marshes in that region than today. (Even today a few colonies of night herons still exist in the riverine woods of the Cher–Indre region, within less than fifty miles of Nohant.) It seems likely that, for the purposes of her fiction, George Sand's imagination transported night herons from the river-lands and marshlands around Nohant to the Normandy coast, without her being aware of the great improb-ability she was creating.

A hundred or more years ago, ornithology was still a

comparatively undeveloped science, and bird-watching – as we know it everywhere today – simply did not exist. (The bird-theme of *Les Ailes de Courage* must have seemed unusual in its own time.) George Sand herself was an impulsive personality with a strong mind, energetic and creative, but certainly not scientific. As a writer, she was copious and rapid, seldom caring to revise, check and correct.

Nothing of an ornithologist myself, I have had to rely on the expert advice of those who are. And I have always had to balance a respect for modern scientific knowledge with a respect for the formidable shade of George Sand herself. I have seldom ventured substantially to alter; but I have often omitted. For instance, George Sand was mistaken when she wrote that, among the night herons, only males bear the white head-plumes. I corrected her mistake by cutting it. Other misinformation, more deeply embedded in the story, I have had to let stand.

But, after all, *Les Ailes de Courage* is a story, not a treatise. Readers have to accept, as Aurore and Gabrielle once accepted, what is told them, and freely give themselves up to a tale of sea-shores and pursuits and hiding-pläces. In return, they will smell the salt of the sea-air and hear the beat of wings overhead and make out the lonely, courageous figure of a little boy scaling the cliffs and dunes in search of a strange fortune.

Philippa Pearce
1981